What Others Are Saying

I admire people who are willing to risk everything, even their own lives, to help the poorest of the poor and tell the untold about God's unconditional love. They are my heroes. Because the poorest of the poor and the ones who have not heard are not found in places we would think about going to for vacations, rather in some of the most un-hospitable places on our planet. Like the Amazon jungle.

JoeLynn's willingness to lay down her life for the cause of Christ and track into the remote regions of the Amazon jungle makes her one of those 'rare breeds" of champions who live life on the cutting edge.

Her sacrifice and courage, her determination as a young woman to beat the odds and do what others said could not be done, takes the reader on a journey that is exciting, adventurous, and inspiring. A must read!

William Turkovich, Missionary to Sierra Leone, West Africa

This is a classic missionary story that throbs with the heartbeat of God for lost souls and lost people, written by one upon whom the Providential hand of God has rested from childhood. JoeLynn Daugherty is what missionaries like to call, "the real deal." She lives and breathes primitive missions. Nurtured and prepared by God over many years for the miraculous ministry into which He has called her, to fulfill a dream that He planted first within her father's heart, and then within her own, JoeLynn has written a story which is brimming with Divine destiny, guaranteed to help you fulfill yours!

Rev. Joseph Purcell, Missionary and Director of Rhema Singapore

On A River Called Never

JoeLynn Daugherty

bush
PUBLISHING
& associates

On The River Called Never
ISBN: 978-0-9836109-5-3
Copyright © 2014 JoeLynn Daugherty

Bush Publishing & Associates books may be ordered at
www.bushpublishing.com or www.amazon.com.

For further information, please contact:
Bush Publishing & Associates
www.bushpublishing.com

Dedication

To my father.

Dad, you were my hero. Thanks for showing me an example of my Heavenly Father's love. You left me a legacy of passion and everlasting commitment to missions. Even in your death, you showed me how to live.

To my mother.

Mom, you are my inspiration. Your unwavering faith and steadfastness are my greatest motivations. I am strengthened and empowered on every mission by your prayers. God knew I was going to need special gifts to fulfill His call, so He gave me you and Dad. Thank you for unconditional love that lights my path on this journey through life.

Acknowledgements

Thanks to Dr. Michael Powell and Dr. James Flavin for encouraging me to write. You gave me the encouragement I needed to get started and the push I needed to see it through. Dr. Powell, I'm sure you are smiling at me from Heaven.

Thanks to Jean Tully, ARNP for mentoring me in medical missions and making my year in Guatemala totally unforgettable.

Thanks to Dr. Leeann Denning for seeing the potential in me. Your "tough love" and gentle pushes throughout nursing school gave me the confidence to graduate and fulfill the dream of becoming a nurse.

Thanks to my "jungle buddies." You all know who you are. I look forward to more jungle adventures with you. We are family!

Thanks to my church family for surrounding me with constant prayer. You are my lifeline.

Thanks to Sherri Powell and Carolyn Redden for your hard work in editing.

A multitude of thanks to God who always causes me to triumph, who has delivered me from pestilence, earthquakes, sickness, disease and many times death. You strengthen me when I feel I can't go on and lead me when I know not where to turn. I will continue On the River Called NEVER until I meet you face to face and hear you say, "Well done!"

Contents

Introduction

It was a hot, humid night in the summer of my fifteenth year. Swinging on a tire hanging in the old oak tree, I stared up into the sky. "God, I'll go wherever you want me to go. I'll do anything you want me to do. I'll be anything you want me to be, but please don't call me to be a missionary. I NEVER want to be a missionary."

I knew God was calling me, but I NEVER believed I could answer that call. I was NEVER well enough, rich enough, nor brave enough to be a missionary. I had only a love for travel. I had a passion for exotic places and colorful people, but I had to resolve to watch them on television from the safety of my living room. I would NEVER see them face-to-face.

Floating down the Amazon, hearing the eclectic sounds of the jungle and smelling fragrances unknown to my senses, I couldn't stop the surge of tears. They flowed as rapidly as the current beneath my canoe. *I'm here. I am really here.* I thought to myself. "Now what, God?"

My mother almost miscarried me at five months. I had birth defects and sicknesses that left me frail as a child, but God had a plan. After He healed me, He made provisions for me to go to Bible College, Missions School and Nursing School. He also sent me to Guatemala for a year as preparation for His plan for my life, a plan that ultimately led me to the Amazon Jungle of Peru.

Standing before an indigenous tribe in a remote village on the banks of the Rio Tigrillo, I gave my testimony. It was not a tale of deliverance from drugs, alcohol, or violent street gangs. It was a testimony of growing up in church and healing.

"God saved me and healed me so that I could travel many days, on four different rivers, to tell you that He loves you. He loves you so much that He sent His only Son to die for you so that you might live." It was necessary for those words to be translated from English to Spanish to their own tribal language. God's love transcended time and distance to break through the language barrier to reach the unreached.

God delivered me from earthquakes, hurricanes, volcanic eruptions, guerrilla warfare, near drowning and disease. He sent an angel to deliver me from a burning bus in Guatemala. Again He sent an angel to save me from tumbling down a hill into the Marañon River during a tropical storm at night.

I'm not sure why God chose me. Surely someone else could do it better. I'm not sure what waits for me around the bend. It's challenging. It's exciting. It's everything I dreamed it would be. There's no place I'd rather be than here On the River Called NEVER.

Chapter One

Stepping off the plane, I follow the crowd through customs and immigrations. I have been here before so I know the routine. As my passport and visa are stamped, and my luggage is searched, I make my way outside to find my contact person. The missionaries I will be working with cannot make it to the city to pick me up, but have arranged for one of their workers to meet me and take me to the first village. They have warned me that it will be a four-hour journey that I will find rather interesting. I believe their exact words were, "A journey you will never forget."

Finally, in the sea of faces I see a sign. Not exactly a sign from heaven, but a homemade sign that reads, "Bienvenidos a Guatemala, Jolin." Although welcoming me in Spanish, and totally misspelling my name, I am comforted by the sight of it. Behind the sign is the toothless smile of a brown-faced man with disheveled, coarse black hair and clothes that hang on his frail little frame. The zipper on his worn-out, green and yellow striped pants is either broken or an insignificant part of his outfit. I walk up to him smiling, exchange greetings and introductions in Spanish and follow him to a dilapidated jeep.

The man tells me in Spanish his name is Miguel del Cielo. *Michael from Heaven*. I think to myself. *He doesn't look like much of an angel to me.* I just giggle to myself as Miguel loads my luggage into the jeep.

I notice the dents in the side of his jeep and hope they are not indicative of his driving ability. As I walk past the bald tires, I pray they will hold up long enough for us to reach our destination. Contemplating the inch of mud, which has dried on the exterior, I figure it is actually holding the Jeep together. It has obviously been there since the last rainy season. There is not a cloud in the sky and the cracked dirt beneath my feet tells me there has been no rain here for several weeks.

As it turns out, the dents in the Jeep are indeed indicative of his driving ability. After several close calls in heavy traffic, running over curbs, barely missing a fire hydrant and a couple of pedestrians, I close my eyes. I clench the handle above the door until my knuckles turn white and pray we make it to the village alive.

The traffic in the city is bumper to bumper, but surprisingly it is moving quickly. A little too quickly from time to time to suit my comfort. I just close my eyes again and pray. There are no speed limits, stop signs are put up for decoration only and drivers pass on both the right and left-hand sides of the road. They continuously make three lanes out of two on the steep, winding, mountain roads.

I am quickly caught up in the drive, which is absolutely breath-taking. I notice we are driving on the Pan American Highway. I discover later that the Pan American Highway is a series of highways nearly 30,000 miles long, extending from Prudhoe Bay, Alaska in North America to the Southern tip of South America. It is the longest stretch of highways in the world. Except for a 99-mile portion in Panama, called the Darién Gap, it is almost possible to drive from Alaska to Argentina! The tiny portion we are traveling here in Guatemala, however, winds around mountain villages with little dark-skinned people in bright, multi-colored, hand-woven "typicals." Typicals is the name for their native clothing. They are going on about their daily lives totally unaware of the stranger in their midst. The plush, dark green carpet of vegetation grows right up to the highway. The flowers bloom year round here in the temperate climate and are vibrant in color. The contrast of multicolored flowers scattered here and there against green foliage reminds me of a patchwork quilt as we speed along the mountain highway.

The air is warm and filled with the exotic fragrance of the tropical blooms just outside the window, which I open due to the not-so-pleasant odor inside. After driving for a couple of hours, Miguel suddenly pulls off at a spot in the road where the mountains seem to divide and the foliage is not so dense.

"Are we here already?" I ask in Spanish.

My escort just laughs and points to a narrow winding path that seems to lead straight into the middle of the mountains. "Great! I'm not wearing hiking boots," I say rather disgustedly.

Miguel looks at me puzzled, "Perdóname, Señorita. No entiendo."

Of course he does not understand. I am talking to myself in English. I tell him that it is not important and motion for him to lead. Miguel straps the large piece of luggage onto his back, and carries the smaller one in his left hand. He wields a machete in his right hand to clear away some vegetation in the path. I insist on carrying my laptop computer. Less than an hour into the hike I wish I had not been so insistent.

The warm air has now become wet and sticky. Perspiration beads that formed on my face and brow are now rolling down my neck and chest. I try wiping them with my handkerchief in between swatting the million mosquitoes, which apparently consider me an all-you-can-eat buffet. I cannot take the time to stop because I am already running to keep up with my guide, who is about five hundred feet ahead of me, and now disappearing around a bend.

The jungle seems remarkably quiet. All I hear, besides my own fast and labored breathing, is the constant snapping of twigs beneath my feet and the hacking of Miguel's machete against the thick vegetation. Occasionally, there is an eerie shriek from some charismatic bird in the trees above us. It's probably some kind of warning to the jungle animals of human invasion. One such shriek is so loud and startling that it stops me in my tracks. I jerk my head in the direction of the noise, expecting to see some ferocious animal charging me, and find nothing but a thick, dark green wall of flora. My guide sees my concern and reassures me that it is just the mating call of the male howler monkey. *Monkey? Sounds more like a gorilla!* I think to myself.

Deeper into the jungle we go, and as we do the vegetation grows thicker and seems to close in around us. Every turn looks like the one before. There are no signs, landmarks or trails in the jungle. I wonder several times how my guide knows where he is going. *Or does he?*

It suddenly grows dark, and I notice the vegetation above is so dense that it makes it difficult for the sunlight to penetrate. It has formed a canopy between the jungle floor and the sky. With no warning it begins to rain. It pours down upon us, soaking us instantly. It has probably been raining for a while, but has taken several minutes to reach us through the dense trees. The showers are sudden, intense and sometimes brief in the rain forest. So, as quickly as the rain pours down upon us, it is over. The trickling of raindrops through the thick vegetation, however, lasted almost an hour. The occasional beam of sunlight, the smell of exotic flowers now wet with leftover rain, and the mist the downpour leaves behind is strangely striking! However challenging this trek through the jungle may be, it will leave an unforgettable barrage of images, emotions and scents that will fill my dreams for years to come.

Aside from the Howler monkeys and exotic birds, all is peaceful on our hike through the floral maze of jungle here in the Petén. I'm thankful we have had no hazardous encounters with any dangerous creatures, especially the slithering kind.

At the end of the path, is a quaint little river with a weather beaten dugout canoe pulled up to the bank. *Ah, my chariot awaits.* I am just thrilled to be off my feet and in a boat where I do not have to watch my every step for creepy critters and slithering snakes. Miguel effortlessly glides into the canoe and steadies it, shifting his weight to balance mine as I slowly and cautiously step down into it. Once I am securely situated in the center of the canoe we shove off. As Miguel swiftly paddles away from the shore, I whisper a prayer that this hollowed out tree keeps us afloat.

"Here we go," I whisper to myself as we push off from the bank and catch a ride on the current of the river. *How would anyone find me in this place?* I wonder. *If only my father and Marlin Perkins could see me now.*

Floating down the river, I notice the jungle around me is bustling with animal sounds and activities. It is filled with fascinating fragrances, and moving in rhythm to the songs of the wild birds. It is quite a contrast to the trek through the jungle that my guide and I just made on foot. The enchanting sounds of the jungle help me forget the hostile look of the river, and the prospect of snakes hanging from the limbs above me. I am nearly lulled to sleep. As I shut my eyes, I can hear the poetic rhythm of the jungle sounds, much like the rhythm of music. In this dreamlike state I begin to contemplate my life and wonder how I ever got here.

As a child, every Saturday night I would stretch out on the floor at my father's feet as we watched that week's episode of *Mutual of Omaha's Wild Kingdom*. Then, as I got older, it was *National Geographic Explorer*. Much to my mother's chagrin, this was a weekly activity that my father and I looked forward to experiencing together. He and I frequently talked about traveling all over the world, but thought the chances of that were slim. We didn't have money for exotic vacations and international travel. However, in spite of our lack of finances, my mother and father made sure we had an annual family vacation. We had a four-man tent that was just big enough for my mother, my father, my brother and me. So, we went camping!

We found a campground with a lake where we could hike, fish and swim. The campground also had a nature center with naturalists that taught about wild animals and plants. They had several animals available for us to see and sometimes hold or at least touch. We were taught which wild plants were edible and which ones were poisonous. One year we even learned how to catch rainwater in case we ever got stranded in the woods without clean water.

It was quite fascinating for a young "explorer" like me. Little did I know at the time that one day those skills would be so valuable. I only dreamed of getting the chance to venture beyond the borders of my own country. My family didn't have the resources for world travel and dreams alone weren't enough to get me to my destination. I would eventually wake up only to find myself in my own boring, insignificant town in rural USA. I would have to settle for viewing the world from afar, through the lens of some cameraman, instead of my own binoculars.

Growing up in church gave me the opportunity to hear many stories from missionaries who lived all over the world. Stories about their lives, the people they ministered to and the dangers they encountered everyday in foreign lands. Soon their words became giant movie screens and I watched those stories from the edge of my seat, in the magnificent color of my imagination. I was enthralled by their encounters with the natives, the different customs and food, and the shock they felt stepping from one culture to another. There were stories of language barriers and struggles with the government and local authorities. Accounts of disease and death. Stories of triumph and tragedies. In the end, it seemed that something in their stories left a dark impression on my fragile mind.

Their stories intrigued me, even held me captive. I was swept away to another land and another people. I was caught up in the drama of their lives, but came crashing to earth at the reality of something I did not recognize at the time. I received mixed signals. I did not want to take advantage of the people I was called to serve, but neither did I want to suffer and die at their hands. I was too young to find glory in being a martyr. No! That was not the life for me. In spite of it all, their stories fascinated me and filled my dreams night after night throughout my childhood.

One summer evening during my sixteenth year, after countless missionary stories, I sat in a swing in my backyard, looked up to heaven and said out loud, "God, I'll do anything you want me to do, be anything you want me to be, and I'll go anywhere you want me to go… in the United States, but please, please don't ask me to be a missionary. I NEVER want to be a missionary!"

At the time, I meant every word. At least I thought I did. I wanted nothing to do with being a missionary. After years of missionary horror stories, I was left to believe that missionaries must be God's stepchildren. According to their accounts, it seemed to me, God would send them over to some foreign land and then forget where He sent them. It was as if God only heard and answered prayers that were prayed in the United States. Once you left the States, sorry, but your prayers were no longer heard.

If for that reason alone, the "wild kingdom" would NEVER be tamed by me. I would leave that up to Marlon Perkins. I would often hold my breath and shut my eyes, as ferocious lions charged unsuspecting villagers on the television screen.

"Did he get 'em?" I would ask.

"No, Sis, he didn't get them," my father would reply. I slowly opened my eyes, one at a time, to see for myself that my father was right.

For years I was content to observe it from the safety of my own house, at my father's feet. Deep inside, I knew there was something more. Much more. God had a plan for me. It would not be revealed for many years, but deep inside… I knew. I dreamed of it. I longed for it.

In high school I took Spanish, not because I was ever going to use it, but because I was going to college to become a nurse or a microbiologist and I needed a foreign language. I chose Spanish. It sounded prettier than German, and French was offered at a time that conflicted with my other classes. Luckily, I enjoyed the class and it seemed that language came somewhat easily to me.

The last day of class before I graduated from high school my Spanish teacher, whom I had known for three years at that point, handed me a piece of paper with a phone number on it.

"Joséfa (my Spanish name), here's my telephone number. Call me someday when you use your Spanish."

I had no idea what she meant, but I tucked it inside my textbook and told her that I would. Ten years and many twists and turns later, I found that textbook with her number in it. After much debate and hesitation, I had accepted the invitation to go on a mission's trip to Guatemala with my parents. I needed to freshen up my Spanish; after all it had been a decade since I had used it. I dialed the number, wondering if it was still hers. Surprisingly she answered and I began to explain who I was.

"Oh, yes, Joséfa. I remember you."

I was shocked that she remembered, but still I managed to answer.

"Well, I haven't used my Spanish yet, but I am getting ready to go to Guatemala next month."

"Guatemala?" She sounded shocked. "What for?"

"Well…" I stumbled over the next few words; "I am going on a mission trip for two weeks to help a registered nurse hold medical clinics out in the small rural villages."

"I should have known you would do something like that."

"Why do you say that?" I was puzzled. There was no way she could have known. At that time in my life I didn't want anything to do with missions. I didn't really want to go on this trip either, but gave in to the nudging of my parents and my missionary friends.

"Because every time we would talk in class about the people and their different cultures you would sit on the edge of your seat. You did well with the grammar part, but you really seemed to come alive when we talked about the people."

"Really?"

"Absolutely. I knew some day you would find your way to a Spanish-speaking country." Then she said something like, "I just never thought it would be a place like Guatemala."

"Trust me, neither did I!"

As we hung up I wondered to myself, *"What did she mean 'a place like Guatemala'?"*

It took a lot to get me to agree to go on this mission trip. I never thought I could afford to go, but my mother and father had been there before and would help me. I figured if Mom could do it, so could I. After all, what could happen with my parents by my side? *I had to ask!*

I was startled as I felt the plane slow and drop altitude. Then the pilot came on to announce that we were beginning our initial descent into Guatemala City. I leaned my head against the window and watched as we flew over the city. The sight of the mountains and dense forest was overwhelming. I overheard a man tell the lady next to him that the airport was built on top of a dead volcano.

"They just leveled off the top of this volcano and built the airport on it," he said with arms acting out his every word.

How do they know that it's dead? And what exactly does a DEAD volcano mean anyhow? I wondered to myself.

The landing was fairly smooth, but I swear the pilot took the turn on two wheels and scraped the wing on the tarmac before we finally came to a stop at the gate. I gathered my carry-on luggage and inched my way off the plane. I followed my parents because they had done this once or twice before. We just trailed behind the passengers in front of us until we got through what looked like cattle gates, which led all of the international passengers to a wide-open room.

There were hundreds of people moving about everywhere like little ants. Hundreds of people were hurrying here and there with little children, luggage and various freight, yet there seemed to be very little noise. The sight of men in fatigues with their fingers gently tapping on the triggers of M-16's was enough to discourage all unnecessary conversation.

Signs hung everywhere directing travelers where to go and what to do. Citizens wait in this line. Foreigners wait in that one. Passports stamped here and immigration over there. Fortunately, the signs were in English as well as Spanish. Being in a foreign country made me uncomfortable enough without having to wonder if I was following the correct procedures. I did not want to make any mistakes in this country.

So there we were, three Americans, amongst thousands of Guatemalans. We completed all of the paperwork, gathered our two duffle bags each and headed toward the doors where our host missionary was waiting to take us on a 4 hour road trip to his home. As we walked toward the doors, we came upon a room with a sign that read "Aduanas." My father leaned over and said, "You don't want to go in there. That's where…" and before he could finish his sentence, we were approached by two armed guards and escorted into the room.

They placed our luggage, the obviously mysterious looking duffle bags, onto the tables and began to ransack them. We had over $60,000 worth of medicines and medical supplies in those bags. You see, my mom knew how to pack. She showed me how to wrap the medicines along with the supplies and bury them in the bottom of the bags. Then she placed a few toys that rattled on top so the custom officials would think that the rattling of the meds were just the toys. I had teased Mom and called her "God's little smuggler." Although none of it was illegal, and we had an official document that permitted us to carry it into the country, in situations like this, it makes no difference. The officials could make up any rule they wanted, confiscate the medicine and supplies and sell them on the black market. Not to mention the bribes they wanted.

Mom whispered to me, "Pray, Sis! Pray they don't dump out the bags and find the medicines."

Being the obedient daughter that I was—I prayed.

Under my breath, but with all of my might I said, *Oh, God, please don't let them dump everything out. Don't let them discover the medicines.*

Even though I was in a foreign country and not in the United States, God must have heard. He must have answered because it was just then that the guard conducting the search, stopped and put the outer garments he removed back into the duffle bag. Then he closed it up. He did not even open the other bags. When the official in charge came over and asked if he had checked everything, he answered, "yes."

That didn't satisfy him though. He wanted some money. He informed us that we had too much luggage and supplies for our trip and wanted us to pay him for the extra luggage. We tried to explain that we were there to work with some missionaries to hold a medical clinic to help his people, but that didn't matter either. He was determined to get some money. So the commanding officer ordered that I go out into the crowd and find the missionary and bring him in for questioning. At that point a guard, armed with an M-16 machine gun, escorted me out the doors to look for the missionary.

In the mean time, the missionary standing on the balcony above us saw the whole thing and was making his way down to the room. I was outside, however, looking for him. After some time the guard grabs my arm and drags me back inside. It was at this time that my imagination ran away with me and I envisioned the three of us in prison like Paul and Silas. Bound hands and feet in shackles. Laying on the cold cement floor of a dark, damp, dungeon. Rats playing "ring-around-the-rosie" at our feet. The smell of rotting flesh filling our nostrils. Fortunately, before my imagination got too carried away I was ushered back into the room with my parents, who were talking with the missionary by this time and about to be released.

I thought the worse was over and since we were finally with the missionary everything would be all right. Well, that's what I get for thinking in English in a Spanish speaking, Central American, under-developed country. I wasn't "in Kansas anymore, Toto," and I needed to hang on for the ride of my life!

Dad, as well as our entire luggage, went in Fred's Toyota 4Runner. Mom and I were placed in the back of a beat up van, with no windows, no air conditioner and driven by a Guatemalan who didn't speak any English and didn't have a driver's license. Well, if he did have one, he must have gotten it out of the bottom of a Cracker Jack box. He ran over several curbs leaving Guatemala City and bounced Mom and I all over the back of that van. A few hours later we weren't sure we would ever see Dad or Fred again, let alone the United States.

There had been a great deal of guerilla warfare months before the presidential election was to take place, and rumors were raging that a coup was imminent. One of the major bridges between the capitol city and the town to which we were headed on the pacific coast had been blown up by the rebels. This made travel between the two cities extremely slow and difficult.

After two long hours, we reached the bridge. Traffic was backed up for miles. One by one, vehicles were motioned to drive through the river to the other side.

It took us an hour to finally reach the river. There were little wooden produce stands with thatched roofs set up along the side of the road. Women and children walked up and down the side of the road selling everything from fried bananas to t-shirts. They were definitely taking advantage of a bad situation and these people were stereotyped as ignorant and lazy. It looked like they were pretty smart to me and definitely far from lazy!

Darkness fell fast as we sat in the back of the van inching our way toward the twisted, jagged metal that was once a bridge. We were warned before we left *never* to travel after dark. It was very dangerous. The words echoed through my head many times as the sky grew darker and darker. My imagination ran wild with me once again until my insides knotted so tightly that my imagination could run no more.

I was so frightened that I wanted to scream at the driver to turn his dilapidated van around and take us back to the airport where we could hop the first flight home to America. Then I remembered, there was only one flight out a week, so I might as well trudge on and see this thing through. Besides, I couldn't let Mom know that I was scared. I didn't want to hear, "Oh, ye of little faith." If ever I needed faith, it was now!

Finally, it was our turn to cross the river. We began our descent down the side of the riverbank and into the water. Because it was the dry season the water was shallow. It seemed as if I could feel every stone we ran over in that riverbed and could almost give you an exact count. *Hang on bladder; it's just a few more feet,* I thought to myself as the urge to relieve myself moved from fullness to pain.

We finally reached the other side and away we went. Our driver obviously felt that he had to make up for lost time, because he drove like he was competing at the Indy 500. Nighttime in Guatemala, on winding mountainous roads, with potholes you could lose a cow in, was no place for Nascar.

After a few more hours of driving, stopping at check points along the way, and bumping around the back of this van with a driver who didn't speak English, we made it to our destination. We were a little worse for wear, but alive and in one slightly battered piece. There were times when the van would stop at a checkpoint and we would hear voices in Spanish all around the van. The back door of the van would suddenly pop open and there would be several men in camouflage clutching tightly to their M-16's, machetes and other weapons of warfare. My heart would drop into my stomach and begin pounding wildly as it tried to climb back up to my chest cavity. Each time the thought would flood my mind, *This is it. They're going to kill us!* Sometimes, an overactive imagination can be very problematic.

It was sometime around midnight when we drove into Retálhuleu, a small town built around a big white Catholic church. This was going to be home for the next two weeks. The streets were narrow and most were one-way. I believe there was only one way into town and one way out. The town was virtually dead, except for the corners where the cantinas were located. They were still hopping with activity. We finally pulled up in front of a big, black iron gate. The driver honked once. Within thirty seconds the iron gate opened and out walked a friendly face. It was Jean, Fred's wife, who came to greet us. Was I ever relieved to see her! There were many times I was sure I would *never* see a familiar face again.

Our luggage was unloaded and mine was taken upstairs to a cinderblock room. I had to share it with a fourteen-year-old Guatemalan girl named Isabel. She didn't speak any English and my Spanish left much to be desired. She was still up. She had waited to meet the

American girl who would be sharing her room. She was pleasant and constantly smiled. It was obvious that at least SHE was glad I was there.

Jean asked if we would like something to eat. I appreciated the offer but replied, "No, thank you. I would just like to take a shower and go to bed."

She understood that it was a long hard trip and that we had been up since four o'clock the previous morning. I actually think she was relieved that we didn't want anything. She was tired too. So, we were welcomed to the missionaries' home and wished a good night. Bath towels had been laid out for me on my bed and instructions on how to use the shower. It was tricky.

Of course it was. Wasn't everything in this country?

The shower was clean, but had a pipe sticking out of the wall from which extremely cold water would run out and send an overheated body into shock. There was a showerhead with wires sticking out that could be attached to the pipe. Bare wires and water, what an extremely electrifying combination! Besides the danger involved we had to learn how to adjust the water. If we ran the water too slow, it got too hot. If we ran the water too fast, it was too cold. There was no spray, just a stream. Well, I wasn't about to figure it out that first night. So, a cold shower it was. But at least I went to bed clean!

I finally climbed into bed and wanted nothing more than to become immediately unconscious. However, one very excited Guatemalan girl wanted to tell me her life story in a language in which I could only understand about every tenth word. I guess she

thought if she repeated the word slowly I would somehow understand it the second time around. All I wanted was to find her power
button and turn her off. She finally said, "Buenas noches," which
I knew meant good night, and she turned off the light.

I had no sooner fallen asleep, and was dreaming I was back in
my own hometown, when the sounds of machine gun fire jerked
me from my sleep and threw me to the floor. I let out a scream as I
rolled underneath the bed. I knew I should *never* have gone there. I
knew my life was over. I wanted to find the cure for cancer and save
the world, but instead my body would be found riveted with bullet
holes, in the fetal position, underneath a bed, in some god-forsaken
town in Central America. This was not how I had imagined my life
was supposed to end.

Suddenly someone interrupted my nervous breakdown by tapping me on the shoulder. I looked up, expecting to see a rebel with
a machine gun, but instead gazed into the eyes of a very confused
14-year-old girl. She was very sweetly trying to tell me something,
which I did not understand.

"Esta bien! Esta bien! Son cuetas!"

I knew *esta bien* meant *it's all right*, but I had no idea what *cuetas*
meant. Besides, machine gun fire was far from all right. She could tell
I did not understand so she tried to show me by acting as if she was
lighting something, throwing it and hearing it pop.

"Grenades? Bombs?"

"No, no bombas, cuetas!"

Well, that night I never figured out what she was saying, but I assumed that if she was not afraid, why should I be? So, I climbed out from under the bed and back into it and laid awake the rest of the night waiting for something else to happen.

What on earth am I doing here? I asked myself over and over again.

The next morning I was awakened early from the precious little sleep I got by the sounds and smells of the world outside. I arrived downstairs long before breakfast was ready and found there was nothing I could do to help except to make myself comfortable. I was too nervous to sit there, wait, and watch someone else work. I had way too much nervous energy. Besides, I knew if I sat still for very long I would be sound asleep!

I did find out, however, that the "machine gun fire" I heard the night before was firecrackers. I was informed that firecrackers are lit and thrown outside of an individual's bedroom window as a means of celebrating his or her birthday. To say the least, I did not share my episode underneath the bed with my hosts and hoped desperately that my roommate would choose to keep quiet about it too.

"Do you mind if I take a walk outside?" I asked my host, hoping to avoid any more conversation of "cuetas."

"I guess it will be all right. Just stick close to the house," Jean answered.

"OK, sure!" And away I went.

I walked through the courtyard, out into the carport and opened the huge iron gate. As I did, I opened the door to a whole new world.

Passing by me were people of different color, different culture, different lifestyles, values and beliefs. On the other hand, upon closer inspection, I noticed they were not all that different from me. They spoke a different language, but there were women feeding their children (okay, so they were breastfeeding them), and men huddled together solving the world's problems just as they did in my local Wal-Mart store. There were boys who were chasing and tormenting girls, and girls who were flirting with the boys.

I stood motionless for a moment, not quite sure what to do. Then one by one I noticed people passing by me smiling and saying, "Buenos Dias!" I said good morning to them too, in their own language and returned their smiles. It made me feel good. I felt like I was accepted by them and I felt as if I were part of their world.

As I started to walk around the block, I was suddenly transported to another world, another time and place. It was as if I had stepped backwards in time. For this country seemed a hundred years behind my own. One block led to two blocks and then three. Before I knew it I was down in Center Square staring at the big Catholic Church and all the statues in the courtyard. Although it was early in the morning, the square was thriving with activity. People were going about their daily lives. There were street vendors, dressed in bright "typical" clothes on the corners selling everything under the sun, most of which I had never seen before. The smell of fresh baked goods filled my senses. I noticed brilliant flowers everywhere. Fragrances and beauty I had never experienced in the States. I heard the bell in the church tower and was immediately made aware of the time.

"*Oh, my gosh! They are going to come looking for me,*" I thought to myself as I headed back toward the mission house.

As I rushed back, I realized that something had happened to me on that walk. My heart had changed. Somewhere between the front gate of the mission house and Center Square my heart began to melt. I realized that I loved this country. I loved these people. I no longer had to believe someone else's stories. I saw for myself that there was life outside my own country. Other people, other cultures, other religions really existed beyond my borders. They were different enough to make them interesting, yet familiar enough to be comfortable around. I learned just enough on that incredible walk to determine that I wanted to know more. I didn't say anything to anyone about my change of heart. I figured I would wait to see what else happened and make sure it wasn't all just my emotions wreaking havoc with me.

That first week my mom and I had the job of helping Jean get ready for the all-day medical clinic coming up the following week. We had hundreds of medicines to inventory, sort and package. Then, each container of medicine had to be labeled with special labels that Jean designed for the clinics. Many of the people in the *campos* and villages could not read or write, so labels were designed with pictures and symbols rather than words.

Since proper nutrition is an issue in underdeveloped countries, vitamins are number one on the list of needed meds for clinics. Literally, tens of thousands of vitamins are dispersed at each of the medical clinics. A variety of vitamins are needed, such as children's chewable, adult, and pre-natal. Jean explained that she usually hands out a 30-day supply of vitamins to every adult and child over 2 years of age. She also gives out enough prenatal vitamins, with folic acid, to get the woman through her pregnancy and three months after delivery because of breastfeeding. Jean made herself available to the patients, so that if they ran out they could always go by the mission house and pick up more vitamins and other needed meds. Jean would council with the expectant and new mothers about childcare and post-partum issues. She would often go around and educate the women and young girls about various aspects of health care and hygiene.

It was a week of long days and tedious work. Nevertheless, it was extremely educational and eventually led to the realization of a lifelong dream. Years later I would remember the days I spent in Guatemala with Jean. Finally, I was convinced that I could follow my heart, go to college and become a registered nurse.

The day of the medical clinic started before dawn. The clinic site was about an hour and half away. Travel was slow because of the road conditions. Over half of the roads we had to travel were dry, dusty, dirt roads that were filled with potholes. Some of the potholes you could drown in if they were filled with water. Thank goodness it was the dry season and rain was not an issue.

Since we had loaded the majority of the medicines and supplies the night before, it didn't take us long to load up and head out. So, by 6:30 a.m. we were on the road to *La Maquina*. The women rode in the 4Runner, while Dad, Fred and one of our interpreters rode in the truck loaded with the supplies.

When we finally arrived, we unloaded the vehicles and began to set up the clinic. There were three doctors from Oral Roberts University doing their internships and volunteering their services at Jean's medical clinic. We sat up chairs to accommodate four medical stations and seating inside the building. The building was a cinder-block, four-sided, open room with no windowpanes, no ceiling, just a metal roof and rafters.

Several dozen people were already lined up outside, waiting to be seen. Most of the people had never been treated by a doctor before. For others, it had been a few years since the last time they were treated or attended a clinic. The people were poor, extremely poor. They couldn't afford doctors or medicines, and surgery was completely out of the question. Flyers had been handed out the week before. Local pastors made announcements to their congregations, and a car with a bullhorn went through the village streets announcing the clinic the following day.

The clinic was set up with the four med stations and a "pharmacy" in the back. The pharmacy was a couple of folding tables that the missionaries brought from home. The donated meds were grouped together and lined up neatly in rows. As the doctors would examine patients and prescribe the meds, they would write a prescription and hand it to the patient to take back to Jean at the pharmacy. She would gather the meds, put them in a bag and then explain how to take the medicine properly. Since Jean was an RN she was familiar with the meds, and because she was fluent in Spanish she could explain it to the villagers in their own language without the use of an interpreter. The interpreters were busy translating for the ORU doctors. Mom and I, we were "winging it."

We had volunteers from the local church to handle crowd control and gather patient information for follow-up purposes. Mom, who did not speak any Spanish was bringing the people in and placing them in the rows of wooden benches waiting to be seen by the doctors. As the doctors would finish seeing one family, she would bring over the next family and keep each station filled and the line moving in an orderly fashion. Not knowing the language, Mom was left to her own creative devices for communication, body language and hand signals. She would wave this person here and motion that person there and physically move another person someplace else.

It got to be rather comical for the locals. Mom would catch movement out of the corner of her eye and turn to see the people imitating her movements and laughing. It was quite amusing to everyone involved. Mom was having fun with them and they were enjoying her. They made the best of the situation by entertaining themselves during their long wait.

I was the one who would get their height, weight and temperature and log the findings on the patient information sheets that each family would take to the stations to see the doctors. It was easier for me in that position because I spoke a little Spanish. Not much, but a little. I would send them to the next row of benches that Mom would pull from to forward on to the doctors, as they were ready. My job, however, was not as easy as it may sound. Since I was not fluent in Spanish at this time, I had to use a little language and a little of Mom's creative techniques.

I especially had difficulty getting my point across to the little children. I would tell them to get on the scales. They would. They would SIT on them. The crowd would roar with laughter. I would desperately try to get my point across by showing the child myself and then repeating the word *stand* in Spanish. Finally, it would work and the child would step up onto the scales and stand. Once, however, I pointed to the scales and the little boy stepped up on it, and immediately began to LOOSE weight. He relieved himself of about a quart of urine onto my scales. To say the least, the entire clinic erupted in laughter. Including me! In a situation like that, it was better to laugh than cry. The progress was halted momentarily while I sanitized the scales for the next child. Jean just giggled and shook her head. She knew I would long run out of sanitizer before the kids ran out of urine!

We worked long and hard at the clinic. It was hot and humid, and there was no air circulating inside the building. The roof was made of metal sheeting. The hot Guatemalan sun beating down upon the tin roof turned the building into an oven. We stood for hours on a cement floor, baking in the stagnant heat of the oven we were working in, but the work was so rewarding. While working at the clinic, none of us thought about how difficult the labor was. It was a service to the people and we could see how much they desperately needed those services. One couldn't help noticing the heat, humidity and bugs. Mainly flies. However, we just wiped away the sweat, swatted at the flies and fanned occasionally with whatever we could find then kept working until the last little person was seen and served.

We broke at noon for lunch. Jean had prepared sandwiches for all of the workers to eat, and there was plenty of bottled water to keep us all hydrated. There was even a "potty" for those who were brave enough to try it or as in Mom's case, for those who were desperate! After Mom's experience with the "potty" I quickly learned to train my bladder.

Fred made the announcement that a "private" toilet was made available for us. After being told earlier that morning to "go now or forever hold your 'pee,'" I was excited at first that a toilet was made available, that is until I laid my eyes and uh, …nose on it. It was no toilet and so I continued to hold my "pee." Thank you anyways! Of course, I did not voice my disgust to anyone. I was there to help mend, not offend.

Mom, on the other hand, was in need of bladder relief and was willing to give it a try. She walked into the outhouse, which was made of corn stalks woven around some wooden poles to represent three walls, and with a sheet of plastic hanging down for the door. There was no roof, which actually turned out to be a blessing because it allowed fresh air to come in and much of the smell to escape.

However, they were a little skimpy on the walls. Mom walked under the blowing plastic "door", and sat down on the bucket, otherwise known as the toilet. Sitting there on the toilet, Mom just smiled as she emptied her bladder into the bucket. I know she was smiling because I saw her. We all could. The walls covered only the bottom half of a standing adult. After being seated, the head and shoulders were still visible. So this was Fred's idea of a private bathroom?

Actually, Fred knew this all along. He planned to get Mom in the bathroom and have all the people standing around to hold a conversation with her. Well, they did. One by one different individuals would begin to ask her all of these questions while she was "on the bucket." Fred was interpreting. Whether or not they were asking the questions that he said they were still remains a mystery. Fred was good at making up stories.

We saw a lot of sick patients in La Maquina. One of the babies we saw was dying from worms. The baby was so infested that the worms were literally crawling out of his mouth and nose. They were choking the life out of him. Worms are easy to treat in the States and something from which no child should die.

I took the temperature of a young lady burning up with fever, who was so weak she could hardly stand. Turns out she had Yellow Fever. Another lady there had black measles. Very serious and very contagious. Not a single one of us volunteers got sick. THAT was a MIRACLE! We saw over 300 patients that day and many good things came out of that clinic.

After we returned home that evening and unloaded the supplies, we were all extremely tired, but also very hungry. Jean was too tired to cook anything and Rosa Linda, their maid, had already gone home for the day. So, we all showered and went to La Colonia restaurante for a late dinner. La Colonia was a fairly nice hotel, with a pool and a restaurant. That is where the missionaries took their guests to relax by the pool and have a nice meal.

We were all so tired that we got "slap happy." We began telling stories about different aspects of our trip, the days leading up to the clinic and different amazing incidents that happened at the clinic. It became hilarious. We laughed until our sides hurt and Jean, who was drinking Coca-cola at the time, laughed with a mouth full of Coke and it went up her nose. We really began laughing then.

"So do you always unwind after each clinic by coming home and snorting Coke?" I asked. We all had a good meal, enjoyed the stories and laughter and then went back to the mission house and collapsed into bed.

The next night we held an evangelistic campaign in that same village. Fred was in charge of the campaigns. Some of the workers in the church, including the pastor, helped Fred with the campaigns. It took a couple of hours to set up all of the equipment. After everything was set up, the pastor of the local village church would usually have the missionaries over for dinner before the service. We never knew what we might get served, but it was always the very best they had.

The campaigns would start off with music. The people of Guatemala and most of the Central American countries are notoriously late. So, Fred would have the music team start playing and lead the people who had gathered together in songs. It wouldn't be long before people starting coming from miles away on foot or bicycles to see what the music was all about.

Then the "Jesus Movie" would be shown to the crowd. The screen was a giant white sheet stretched out between trees, poles, buildings or whatever else could be found. The image could be seen from both sides and it could be heard for miles. By the time the movie was over and the lights came on the crowd had multiplied greatly. There were people as far as the eye could see.

I looked around and noticed that there were people in trees, hanging on fences, and on rooftops watching and listening to every word that was spoken. After the movie someone gave the message from the Bible and the call for prayer. It was amazing to listen and watch, and very emotional for me to observe. To think, I *never* wanted to be a part of any of this!

Toward the end of the service, Mom and I noticed the little girls standing around us. They kept walking up asking to touch Mom's hair. Her hair was silky, soft and snow white. The people there had thick, coarse, coal black hair. So Mom's hair was a bit of a novelty. They all, men, women and children alike, wanted to touch her hair. They figured she had to be ancient to have such white hair, but several said that her skin was so smooth and wrinkle free for her to be so old. My mom was snow white headed at an early age, but they thought she must be about a hundred years old.

By the end of the service, several of the little girls had gone home to put flour in their hair. When they returned their hair was as white as Mom's. They were so proud of their accomplishment. Mom loved it! She had such a wonderful time with the girls. It was the end of the service and the mothers were beginning to gather up their children to leave. Mom had found a friend with this one little girl who had climbed up on her lap and sat for much of the service. When it was time for the little girl to go home with her mommy, she started to walk away and then turned to smile at Mom. Mom smiled and waved. The little girl came back and looked up at with her coal black eyes. Mom hugged her and said "adios" and the little girl walked away again. She turned once again and smiled at Mom. Mom smiled and waved again. Once again the little girl came back and stood in front of Mom and looked up at her as if she was expecting something. Her little black eyes staring at Mom wondering. Mom hugged her again and told her good-bye and the little girl left again. This time Jean leaned over and said, "Don't wave to her again. The way we move our hands to say good-bye in the States is the way they motion for someone to 'come' in Guatemala."

We all laughed. The poor little girl had just been trying to go home and Mom kept motioning for her to come back, because she thought she was waving good-bye.

It was during the second week of my first mission trip to Guatemala that I knew I had to come back, I just didn't know when. Jean had invited me to come back and stay a year with them.

A year? Why not? After all, I'm single, with no children, and currently not very happy with my job in retail.

At the end of my two weeks in Guatemala I realized so much within me had changed. The heart that so wanted to serve God, but had said it *NEVER* wanted to be a missionary, was now broken; broken because it was leaving the people and the country it had suddenly grown to love. That frightened, young lady who crawled out from under the bed the first night was now boldly proclaiming her desire to return and become a part of this country. A part of these people.

I was very quiet on the return trip home. By the time I arrived home I was miserable. Three days later, I knew I was going back for a year. Just four months after I arrived home, I was spending the last night with my parents before I left the next morning for Guatemala. I would be staying with Fred and Jean and their infant daughter. Fred was going to be flying up to the States, picking up a van that was being donated to their ministry, and driving on to Ohio to pick up me and all of my belongings.

I had sold just about everything I owned to get the money to go. I was taking just enough clothes to get by with, a year's supply of toiletries (I didn't want to buy that kind of stuff down there) and my bedding. Oh, yea, and a ceiling fan! We loaded up the van the night before so we could get up early and go.

Mom had also gathered up some more medical supplies and medicines for our next medical clinic. Since Jean was a registered nurse, part of her ministry to the people of Guatemala was holding free medical clinics. Many times the sick even came to her house for treatment or to see if she had medicine to give them when they couldn't afford to see the doctor or have their prescriptions filled.

Mom had also put together a "care package" for the missionaries and one for me. The packages consisted of things that missionaries absolutely love, but can't get on the foreign field. The requested items included the following:

1. Peanut butter (usually number one on every missionary's list)
2. Jelly (variety of flavors, but grape is the only one for me)
3. Macaroni and cheese
4. Cake mix and canned icing
5. Kool-Aid (variety of flavors)

6. Candy bars (Snickers and Butterfinger for Fred and Jean)

7. Various spices that cannot be purchased in Guatemala

Then there were the non-food items requested like soap, shampoos, sandwich bags, garbage bags and the ever-loving twist ties, which are handy for a multitude of purposes on the mission field. With twist ties, we missionaries could make even MacGyver look like a novice. I remember a request from one missionary friend living in Africa for hair color and perms. He had a wife and two daughters! Oh, yea, there were also those feminine things. They were not easy to come by in certain countries and if they were available, you would rather they weren't. Most products were by no means the same quality products as they were in the States.

In preparation for my year in Guatemala, I purchased a couple of cases of toilet paper from Sam's Club. I had hoped it would be a year's supply, but after a couple of battles with "Montezuma's Revenge" and a month long bout with Giardia, the supply ran out long before the year was up. Toilet paper in Guatemala disintegrates the very second it comes into contact with moisture of any kind. Let your own imagination paint the rest of the picture.

The next morning came even more quickly than I imagined. It was time to kiss Mom and Dad goodbye for a year. I had already told my church family goodbye. My best friend and I cried all night long the night before. Surprisingly though, it wasn't as hard as I thought it would be. Somehow I knew I was doing what I was supposed to do and that everything was going to be all right. I also knew that in a couple of months Dad was going to come down to visit and then Mom was coming down to visit for my birthday in December and leaving just before Christmas. I actually had no idea what all I had to look forward to and how my life would change in the year ahead. The timid and sheltered little girl was coming back a bold, confident woman.

The trip across the States was interesting, but uneventful. The first night we spent in Louisiana. I got to eat some authentic Cajun food for the first time in my life. That was exciting. We crossed over the swamps and I watched out the window for alligators. It was really quite an interesting experience for me. I was driving through states I had never been in and seeing several things I had never seen before. I didn't realize when I left that this trip was going to be so educational and CHALLENGING!

We arrived in Brownsville, Texas late in the afternoon of the second day. Since it was getting late, we were going to get a hotel room and spend the night on the U.S. side of the border. I was informed by Fred that traveling across Mexico after dark is neither a safe nor a smart thing to do. We also needed to get my visa to cross Mexico. So, we got a couple of hotel rooms, freshened up from the trip and took a drive across to South Padre Island to eat at a restaurant called Miguel's. It was wonderful, authentic Mexican food.

The island was beautiful. The sunset was breathtaking. The sky was pink, purple, yellow and blue. There were small white, puffy cumulus clouds that had turned multi-colored as the sun sank below the horizon. The colors reflected off the calm ocean waters like a piece of polished brass. I was in awe as I walked along the white sandy beaches. It was a lovely ending to a long, monotonous day. Now, it was time to get a good night's sleep for the long, rough drive ahead of us. First thing tomorrow, we were crossing the border into Mexico, driving as far as Pozo Rico, staying the night and then driving through to Guatemala the next day. Such was the plan.

Chapter Two

The sound of the telephone ringing interrupted my dream. It was the wakeup call I had requested the night before. There was a single beam of sunlight shining through the curtains splitting my room in half. I was on one half and the door was on the other. In one brief moment I saw that line of sunlight as the threshold of the new life that was laid out before me. I could stay on the safe side of the line or I could crossover it and open the door to a whole new world. I had come this far. I might as well see what was on the other side of the door.

I jumped up and hopped into the shower thinking I needed to enjoy this one for I was not sure when my next hot, high-pressured shower would be. I wanted to linger there in that shower much longer allowing the hot water to massage the aches away, but I made it quick. We had much to accomplish before crossing the border to my new life.

Before we crossed over, Fred decided to go to a grocery store and pick up a few food items for our trip. We had a cooler in the van sitting on the floor between the front seats. Fred knew that there were very few places we could stop to eat along the way. This was also going to be our last opportunity to buy any needed American goods. So, once again Fred decided to make another stop. This time it was a Wal-Mart.

By the time we bought groceries, ice for the cooler, and the needed items from Wal-Mart we were both extremely hungry. So, we paused to grab some lunch. Afterwards, we went to get travelers' insurance to cross Mexico.

Due to all of the paperwork, and a large number of people who wanted travelers insurance to drive across Mexico, we were late getting away from the insurance office. It was after 4:00 in the afternoon when we finally arrived at the border. However, there was one bit of very important business that Fred forgot to tend to before we got to the border, my VISA! It is impossible for me to get across the border without it.

It was too far to drive into downtown Brownsville to the embassy. It was almost 5:00. Closing time. The only other alternative was to get a taxi to take me across the border to the Mexican embassy. Fred found a young Mexican boy, paid him to accompany me to the Mexican embassy and to speak on my behalf to get my visa.

Fred had to stay on the Texas side of the border with the van. If he crossed and I could not get my visa, then I would be sent back to Texas and Fred would have to stay in Mexico for 72 hours before he could get another visa to cross Mexico. It was a chance that Fred was not willing to take. So, the only thing left to do was to send me to get the visa. If I was denied I would be sent back across the border and we would have to wait until Monday morning. It was now Friday evening and ten minutes until closing.

We were at the border of Mexico. Fred hailed a taxi, spoke to the driver and then told me to get in and go with these two strange Mexican males, which did not speak English, across the border to Mexico to the embassy so that I could cross Mexico into Guatemala. It did not make any sense to me. Nevertheless, off we went to Mexico. I turned to glance at Fred as we pulled away. The thought entered my mind; *you may never see Fred or the United States again.*

I no sooner shook off that horrible thought when we hit something. I heard and felt the impact as we drove over whatever it was. The taxi driver and young boy laughed as they looked into the rearview mirrors. I immediately turned to see what we hit. I wish I hadn't. I turned to see the remains of a dog flopping around in the road. I quickly jerked my head back around. *These people have a very sick, warped sense of humor.* I thought to myself. *Oh, what have I gotten myself into?*

We pulled up to the embassy and rang the bell. A voice came over the speaker box, and Carlos, the young man sent to be my voice, spoke a couple of minutes with the mystery man inside the box. An armed guard appeared out of nowhere. Soon my paid escort motioned me out of the taxi. As I walked toward the huge wrought iron gate I heard a click and it began to open. The guard, who obviously took his job very seriously, led us into the embassy.

I noticed that there was no one around. I glanced up at a giant grandfather clock in the corner of the lobby. It was now 5:10 p.m. *Oh, no! It's too late. Now what do we do?*

The building, although quite old, was immaculate. It smelled musty, but it was clean. The décor was antique, Latin and very military. It actually took on the appearance of a palace. There was dark, extravagantly carved wood, which outlined the windows, doorways and floors. The floors and countertops were magnificent marble. Cathedral ceilings allowed an ominous sounding echo to resound throughout the corridors whenever doors were shut.

Lining the corridors were portraits of past presidents, ambassadors, and military leaders. Every few feet there was a four foot white column with the bust of some dignitary on it. It looked more like a museum or art gallery than an embassy. Then again, I had never been in an embassy before so I had no clue what one looked like.

The guard seated us across from a very large, intimidating desk and then proceeded to walk out without a word. Of course, the door slammed, I jumped, and the echo resounded throughout the corridor again. Before the echo had a chance to completely stop, the ambassador's clerk burst through the door and slammed it shut.

I jumped again.

He laughed.

Then he apologized, in broken English, for startling me. He introduced himself as he shook my hand. He never offered his hand to Carlos. He asked me a few questions pertaining to my visit. Purpose of trip. Final destination. Business or pleasure. Length of stay. Then he stamped it several times and handed it to me with a sheepish grin. I thanked him and turned to look at Carlos expecting to see him move toward the door. Instead, I heard the voice of the clerk reminding me that he stayed past closing time to do me a tremendous favor. His hinting was not very subtle at all.

Oh, my gosh! He wants a bribe. I thought to myself. *But I don't have even a penny. Fred has all my money back in the van across the border.*

While I was having a mini nervous breakdown again in my head, my paid escort realized the situation and paid the clerk $10 US dollars. He gave him the money that Fred had given him to escort me there in the first place. The clerk thanked me for being so generous in my gift and wished me a safe trip. Carlos tapped my shoulder and headed out of the door. The armed guard escorted us out of the embassy and off of the property.

The taxi driver waited for us, just as Fred had asked. He and Carlos talked quietly all the way back to the border. They were probably discussing what happened back at the embassy. Every once in awhile the driver would look back at me through his rearview mirror. I could only imagine what they could possibly be saying about the stupid, ill-prepared American girl who had absolutely no business living in Central America. Then again those were the thoughts going through my own head.

As the taxi neared the Texas border, I could see Fred waiting on the other side. What a sight for my sore eyes. There were a few moments when I questioned if I would ever see him again. I waved and flashed him a smile of relief. He told me later that he knew from my smile I had my visa in hand. He was right. All was well in the world again. At least my world, and at least at this particular moment in time.

I explained to Fred what Carlos had done for me back at the embassy by giving the clerk his ten dollars. Fred gave him some more money. I hugged him and had Fred thank him for taking such good care of me. Everything that transpired during that trip to the embassy stuck in my mind. I thought long and hard about what some young, adolescent Mexican boy did for a strange American young lady. I was willing and ready to forgive him and the taxi driver for their morbid sense of humor at laughing over the poor dog!

They stopped every car that went through to ask questions about the destination of the vehicle and to check legal papers. Some of the vehicles they stopped to search the contents. We were one of the lucky ones that got stopped and searched. They saw a van and figured it is loaded with "contraband."

Fred explained to the border patrol that he was a missionary and that I was going to be visiting Guatemala for a year and was carrying my personal belongings along. They listened to his story as they went through each and every box, suitcase and bag that I had brought. Once in awhile they would pull something out and ask what it was and for what was it used. After what seemed like forever, we were motioned through and were on our way once again across Mexico.

This is it. No turning back now. I thought to myself.

The drive alternated back and forth between boring and exciting. For miles it was like much of Texas. Flat. Dry. Barren. Wasteland. Then there would be quaint, colorful little towns filled will fascinating people hurrying around here and there with all sorts of things carried on their heads and backs. Buses, filled beyond capacity with men, women, children, produce and animals, darted in and out of traffic, honking their horns and filling the air with the smell of diesel.

The buses were obviously "hand-me-downs" from the United States. I heard someone say once that after they no longer passed inspection in the States, and were deemed unsafe for U.S. roads, they were sold to Mexico and Central America. I didn't know if that was true or not, but those buses made it look true. The buses were then "fixed up" and put to good use. "Fixed up" usually consisted of a bright multi-colored paint job and radical accessories. A name was painted in bright contrasting colors across the front of the bus above the windshield. Many of the buses were named. I found this scene to be a common one in every town I drove through in Mexico and Guatemala.

Every once in a while I caught glimpses of the Gulf of Mexico. We took the coastal route. It was a beautiful sight each time I witnessed it. Sometimes it was still, other times there were white caps and waves rolling in and crashing on the shore. After hours of bouncing around in the hot van, I longed to jump out and run head long into the ocean and let the waves crash over me. There was no time for that though. We had to get to Guatemala as soon as we could. Fred had pressing matters he had to tend to there.

The combination of rough roads filled with enormous potholes, a van loaded down with supplies, and tires that were less than new was the recipe for blowouts and stress headaches. It was a good thing we had a couple of spare tires and found a tire place that could not only patch tires, but sold them too. The first day crossing Mexico we blew two tires. We would hit rough road causing the van to start bouncing, and then … BOOM! Blowout!

By the time we reached Poza Rica, our first stop in Mexico, I had a headache that was near migraine proportion. I was nauseated, tense, and had no desire to eat. I just wanted to take some pain reliever, a shower, and go to bed. In that order. However, I settled for taking some *aspirina,* a sponge bath (there was no hot water or shower), and then lying down on something they called a bed, but felt more like plywood covered with sand paper. Nevertheless, I was off the rough roads, out of the van and now horizontal. The pain let up enough so that I could fall asleep just in time to wake up and start all over again.

We were on the road just before dawn. I was a little rested and tried hard not to allow myself to get so worked up that I got another headache. Daylight brought new adventures. We had stops along the way for periodic checkpoints. Those were mini interrogations by the police. They checked for correct papers, and then went through each vehicle and made sure no one was carrying illegal drugs, weapons or anything else suspicious. I guessed that was a good thing, but after the fourth or fifth time we had to stop and wait for them to rummage through my personal belongings and make an even greater mess of them than the last check point made, I was not so sure anymore.

Sometime around mid-morning of the second day of our crossing we drove across a line in the road with a sign saying it was the Tropic of Cancer. I had never been out of my own country before and now I was crossing the 23° 30' parallel line north of the equator. I was entering the tropic zone, where the sun was directly overhead at noon. I found that to be fascinating.

I'm going to have to tell Dad about this. I thought to myself.

The second day of crossing Mexico was much better than the first. We had no more blown tires, so I relaxed my white knuckled grip on the door handle and actually enjoy the sights and sounds of Mexico. We were now following the coastline of the Gulf of Mexico. It was so picturesque, like a postcard.

Suddenly, the sky turned bright orange, then fluorescent pink and purple with small white puffy clouds scattered here and there. It was the most beautiful sunset I had ever seen. The formation of the clouds, and the silhouette of jagged mountains against the backdrop of a pink and purple sky was a Monet come to life. Then reality interrupted my fantasy tour of God's art gallery. This sunset, as beautiful as it was, meant night was falling. Darkness was nearly upon us and we were still driving with no mention of a stop for the night.

The last bit of light was gone. Darkness had enveloped the Monet painting of sunset like a dark cloak. Then Fred pulled over to the side of the road. *Surely we can't just stop here, in the middle of nowhere for the night.* I thought to myself.

"I know it is night, and I told you that we shouldn't and wouldn't drive after dark, but I know this quaint little town just about a half hour further with a nice, clean place to sleep. Would that be all right with you?" Fred asked.

"Whatever you think. You know best," I answered and flashed him a hesitant smile.

"I just have to make a quick, pit stop here and then we can go on." Then he disappeared around a big bush.

After what seemed like an eternity, Fred reappeared, jumped back into the van and away we went. It wasn't ten minutes later that we were stopped once again by the police for yet another mini interrogation. This time was the most frightening stop for me. It was the first time it happened after dark. There were just two small lanterns that gave very little light. The military patrols made us get out of the van. That had never happened before. What would they do with us? What would happen next? There was quite a bit of talk between Fred and the men, none of which I understood, and then it was over. Fred jumped back into the van and away we went.

Just like Fred had said, about twenty minutes later I saw lights up ahead. Fred said something about the lights being the town where we would be staying. I was so excited. I just wanted out of the van for a while. We had been traveling for four days at this point. I had not showered in three. Now I was ready to get to this hotel that had a shower and crash for the night. *How much further do we have to travel before we reach Guatemala?* I asked myself.

There in the midst of the town was a big white Catholic church. There was one in nearly every town we passed along the way, but this one looked identical to the one in Retalhuleu. Then we rounded the corner and there was this familiar looking black iron gate. Fred stopped in front of it and honked. In a few seconds, out walked Jean. I quickly turned my head to look at Fred. I opened my mouth to ask him a really dumb question, when he said with an ornery grin...

"Welcome Home!"

What I failed to realize was that the last police checkpoint was actually the border patrol between Mexico and Guatemala. The papers that Fred showed the patrol were our immigration papers and we crossed over into Guatemala. He had tricked me, but I was so glad he did! I was more than ready to be out of the car and on solid ground. Jean was such a welcoming sight for my tired eyes.

Chapter
Three

I slept soundly the first night and didn't wake up until after 8:00a.m. I knew I was wiped out when I finally got into bed around 1:00a.m. I don't remember much of anything after my head hit the pillow. I think I passed out from sheer exhaustion.

It didn't matter that the sheets on the bed felt like sand paper, or that the temperature in the room was around 80 degrees with about 95% humidity. This time I had my own room with my own bathroom. I didn't hear the rooster just over the cinderblock wall in the neighbor's yard crow all night. I didn't hear the "cuetas" going off at 4:00 a.m. in the next block. Nor did I hear the music that played loudly all night in the apartment over the shop across the street.

I only heard the familiar voices of family and friends, which kept me company in my dreams all night. They continually reassured me that I was going to have the time of my life and experience a lifetime of memories in just one short year. Yes, they kept telling me over and over again that this year was going to go by so fast that I would be home before I realized it. I didn't know how fast that first night's dream was going to come to pass. Nor did I realize how soon I was to start experiencing "life in Guatemala."

As I awoke, I heard voices downstairs and smelled the aroma of breakfast in the making. I was embarrassed that I had slept so late. I quickly threw on some clothes, walked down the cement steps, through the courtyard, and into the dining room. It was there that I was greeted with several friendly, smiling faces.

"¡Buenos dias!" they said in unison.

"¡Buenos dias!" I answered back with a smile.

"I hope you're hungry." Jean said removing the cover on several dishes, which were covered to keep the heat in and the flies out.

There, spread out on the table before me, was scrambled eggs, chorizo, frijoles, shredded cheese, fried platanos and tortillas.

"Rosa Linda prepared a typical Guatemalan breakfast this morning in honor of your first day in Guatemala." Jean informed me.

"Gracías, Rosa Linda," I said thanking the maid for all the work she had done and her thoughtfulness.

Although I was not used to eating breakfast, I enjoyed it and the conversation with Fred, Jean, and an occasional sentence or two with Isabel and Rosa Linda. I soon got accustomed to eating at least a little something for breakfast each morning before going out into the heat, humidity and excitement of the day. It didn't take long before a good hardy breakfast was routine. It jump-started my day.

Fred and Jean gave me a few days to get a little more familiar with life in a foreign country then it was time for the initiation. One day during my second week in Retalhuleu (Reu for short) Fred decided it was time.

"Joe Lynn, we believe in the 'sink or swim' method around here. So, I am going to send you to the panadería this morning. I think you're ready," he said with a grin.

"OK, if you say so," I said a little reluctantly.

"Oh, it's easy. Just walk up the street to the panadería, walk up to the counter and order a dozen gusandas, a dozen besitas and a dozen tostadas. Got it?" he asked in a matter of fact manner.

"Ummm. OK." I wasn't so convinced. But I took the money he was handing me and headed for the metal door.

"Oh, Joe Lynn, wait just a minute," he said running out to the metal door to stop me before I got away. "I would like eggs for break-fast this morning. So, would you order me a couple of "pedos?"

"A couple of what?"

"Pedos."

"How do you spell that?" I asked. I figured if I had the correct spelling, then I would be more apt to pronounce it correctly.

"I think it is p-e-d-o," he said with a convinced look on his face.

"Two?" I asked.

"Yea, a couple will be fine," he said with a straight face.

"OK." I said and I turned to head out the door to the panadería. *My first full week here in Guatemala and I'm already on my first mission.* I thought to myself as I headed up the street.

As I approached the little bakery I could see that it was packed with ladies in bright, multicolored, hand-woven skirts called "typicals." I later discovered that the day Fred sent me to the bakery was the very day that the indigenous people come down from the mountain villages into town to go to market and buy breads at the bakery. He knew that day was going to be crowded.

As I walked into the store I noticed that the crowd parted all the way up to the counter. The lady behind the counter looked back at me and asked if she could help me. That much I understood. I looked around at everyone else who had been in front of me. They all just motioned for me to go up to the counter.

"Pase adalante" several of the ladies said to me, "go ahead."

I don't know why they were all being so nice and allowing me to go first. But, OK. So, I walked up to the counter and smiled big at the lady.

"May I help you?" she asked me, only she asked me in Spanish.

I asked for a dozen of each of the three kinds of bakery items Fred had told me to order. I had practiced how to say them all the way down the street to the bread store. This was my first assignment and I really did not want to mess it up. Now it was time to order the special item he wanted with his eggs.

"¿Qué mas?" she asked. "*What else?*"

"Yo quiero dos pedos." I asked. Immediately laughter erupted in the tiny little shop I was sure it could be heard back at the mission house. Everyone in the shop was laughing except me. I was so embarrassed. I obviously said it wrong. So, when the lady said, "excuse me" I had only one thing to do…say it slower, louder and more pronounced.

"Yo quiero (I want) dos (two) PEDOS!"

Once again laughter exploded in the bakery until women were bent over, slapping their knees, and pointing at the "gringa" who obviously didn't know their language. The lady behind the counter was trying hard to contain her laughter. She obviously felt sorry for me, and my big blunder tried to help me out.

"Do you mean 'huevos' (eggs)?" she asked.

"No, PEDOS!" I blurted out.

"No, sorry," she finally said handing me the bag of other items I had successfully ordered.

I thanked her anyways, turned and walked out trying hard not to make eye contact with anyone else in the shop. There was still laughter roaring as I left the building, which got louder as I walked away. I can only imagine what the conversation was like after I left, but I bet this "gringa" was the topic of that conversation. I suddenly felt the urge to run. I ran back to the metal door of the mission house. As soon as I was safe inside, I slammed it and hollered, "Fred!"

"What did you do to her, Fred?" Jean hollered.

"I don't know. What do you mean?" Fred asked so innocently.

"What did you have me order?" I asked.

"I don't know. Maybe I gave you the wrong word. Let's look it up in the dictionary," he said without cracking so much as a smile. He hands me the Spanish-English Dictionary. I look it up. There, before my very eyes, in big, black letters, was the word p-e-d-o, pedo. It was a noun and a verb. The actual definition the Spanish/English dictionary gave was…f-a-r-t, fart. Fred sent me to the bakery to order two FARTS!

As soon as the reality of the word I was reading set in, I looked up at Fred with eyes as big as silver dollars, and a mouth dropped open to my chin. Fred looked at me, just waiting for a reaction. What I gave him I don't think he was ready for however. I quickly glanced at Jean and ran upstairs to my room, slamming the metal door behind me.

As I threw myself on the bed in total disbelief of the embarrassing situation I had just experienced, I could hear a very loud voice downstairs. It was Jean. She was giving Fred the "fifth degree."

"I can't believe you did that to her. It is one thing to tease the guys like that, Fred, but you can't treat a girl like that. What if she calls her mom and dad and tells them what you have done to her. What if they get upset and send her a ticket home. Even worse, what if they drop our support? Then what will we do?" she drilled him.

All Fred could get in was an occasional, "Uh, I…uh."

"What were you thinking?" she continued.

"Uh, I don't know."

"That's just it, Fred, you weren't thinking. Now, you march yourself up there right this minute and apologize to her."

In the meantime, I got so into the tongue lashing downstairs, that my humiliation disappeared and I went into the bathroom and sat on the toilet underneath the window above the courtyard where the thrashing was taking place. I had to put my hand over my mouth so that neither of them could hear my giggles. The verbal beating Fred received downstairs outranked my humiliation. And I was enjoying it immensely!

It wasn't long, however, before I noticed that the voices stopped and there was a knock at my door. It was Fred.

"Joe Lynn, it's me. I need to talk to you," he said very humbly.

"Go away!" I shouted in my most unpleasant voice.

"Please, open up. I really need to talk to you."

"Well, I don't really feel like talking to you, right now," I continued pitifully. However, it was very hard to keep sounding so angry or hurt.

"Joe Lynn. I am very sorry. I never meant to hurt you. I was just playing a little joke on you," he tried to explain.

"Well, it wasn't very funny. I have never been so humiliated in my entire life. I can't face those people again." I was really laying it on thick. Jean was downstairs adding to his guilt.

"I told you, Fred. Guys may think that kind of thing is funny, but women don't."

Still he tried. "Joe Lynn, would you please open the door and let me explain and apologize to you in person."

I had to put on a serious face and my best acting shoes. This was going to be difficult. I couldn't let Fred off the hook this easy. Slowly I opened the door. Fred was standing at the balcony looking down at Jean. He turned when he heard the door creak.

I walked over to him looking down. Trying to still appear embarrassed or sad. I finally said, "So what do you need to talk about?"

"I really need for you to understand that I never meant to hurt you. I was just playing around. I love to tease and I guess I just don't know when to stop. Would you please forgive me?"

"Of course I will forgive you," I said as a matter of fact. However, he was not getting off that easy. I still remember what he did to Mom with the "private potty" episode and other jokes he pulled on Dad and I during our family trip just a few short months ago. No, he was going to have to suffer just a little more than that.

"Oh, thank you. So no harm done? You aren't going to call your Mom and Dad about this?" he asked hesitantly.

"I said I forgive you, Fred. I did not say that there was no harm done. I also did not say that I wasn't going to call Mom. That is exactly what I intend on doing," I said in my best acting voice.

His face went white and his eyes got big as saucers. "Oh, no, no. Please don't call your Mom. I said I was sorry. I promise I won't ever do anything like that to you again. Please, give me another chance. I will make it up to you." He was grovelling at this time and Jean was pacing downstairs saying, "I knew it! I knew it! You really blew it now, Fred. You really crossed the line this time."

Well, between the look on Fred's face, the panic in his voice and the double whammy he was getting from Jean and me both. It was all I could do to keep from cracking up. I was on the verge of laughter when finally I said to keep from losing it, "All right. All right. I won't call home this time and I will give you another chance, but let me make myself clear, Fred, I will get even with you."

Fred stopped suddenly and looked me square in the eyes. "What?"

"You heard me. I'm no longer mad or hurt at you. But I am going to get even with you. Two can play this game. If I have to take this kind of joking from you then, by golly, I will dish it out too. So, consider yourself warned. I will get even when you least expect it."

Fred grinned from ear to ear. He loved to joke. He knew he was reprieved and to him this was a challenge. A sort of champion of wits contest. Little did he know that he had met his match.

He stuck out his hand and said, "Deal!"

I shook it and said, "Let the payback begin."

Fred treaded lightly for the first few days. Every day he kept expecting me to do something to get even with him. No. That was too easy. He was expecting it. I was going to let it go long enough for him to let his guard down. Then, when he least expected, …POW! I was going to hit him hard. I had no idea what I was going to do yet, but it had to be good. After a few days, Fred forgot about the payback promise and how close he came to losing the support of good friends in Ohio and went back to his old ways of practical jokes and tormenting.

"That's all right," I said one day to Jean over breakfast after Fred had jumped out of the bush at the bottom of the steps from my room. "I'll settle the score one day."

"You're an extremely good sport, Joe Lynn," Jean answered. "A lot more forgiving than I would be."

"Oh, I can take it, but Fred is going to be very surprised when suddenly I dish it out." We both laughed and went on about the day.

A few months later, a week before Fred's fiftieth birthday, I got with Jean to plan my revenge. She was totally on board with the plan. Fred parked his vehicle inside the main gate at night. Theft was a real problem in Reu. Many vehicles had been stolen so he also had an alarm installed. Around 3:30 in the morning of Fred's birthday the alarm went off on his Forerunner. He came flying out of his bedroom and out into the courtyard. The driver's side door was wide open. Armed with a baseball bat, he reached the vehicle with the bat held high, ready to swing. He stopped in his tracks and dropped the bat. There in the driver's seat was a big sign that read, "Happy Birthday, You Old Pedo!" I was standing above him hanging over the balcony laughing. He looked up and smiled, "Good one!" Then his eyes got big, his mouth dropped open and he ran back into the house to his bedroom. He suddenly realized he was standing there in only his underwear. That made the revenge even sweeter!

A few hours later, when we were all seated at the breakfast table, laughter broke the momentary silence. Jean had shared the early morning excitement with Rosa Linda. She too laughed with the rest of us.

"That was the best practical joke anyone has ever played on me, JoeLynn," Fred said with a big grin on his face. "So, now we are even!"

"Oh, not even close, Fred! The revenge has just begun."

"What? Why?" he asked perplexed.

"That does not come close to all the other practical jokes you have played on me. That settles the Pedo score only!" I laughed and winked at Jean.

"She's right, Fred," Jean said winking back at me.

Fred would have to wait until my return to the States for the final installment of revenge.

I had arrived in Guatemala during dry season. It was hot and sometimes got even hotter! It was the tropics, so of course it was humid. That is a given. Jean had suggested before I moved down there to bring a ceiling fan with me. Boy, was I glad I listened. It helped considerably to circulate the extremely hot air around my room. Well, at least it was better than extremely hot and stale air.

Three weeks after my move to Retalhuleu I had started to adopt a new way of life. Early to bed, after all it got dark around 7:00 in the evening. Early to rise, it was bright and sunny by 6:00 a.m. and three showers a day. One in the morning to start the day fresh and to remove the perspiration you acquired during the night. One, in the middle of the afternoon to lower your body temperature a few degrees, and remove the dirt and grit. And then one at night to again lower your body temperature, remove the dirt, and to be able to crawl into bed knowing that you were clean.

I had worked hard one day and was exhausted. After a delicious dinner of BBQ chicken, baked potatoes and the most delicious salad I had ever eaten I went upstairs to shower, write a letter back home, and collapse into bed. It was a very still, hot, and humid Thursday night. Just a few minutes after midnight, I was suddenly and violently jerked from my sleep. I felt a thud, as if someone had picked up the bottom of my bed a couple of feet off the ground and dropped it to the floor. Then the bed began to shake. My first thought was… Fred. Fred is playing another one of his tricks on me.

"Fred, stop it!" I said out loud. Sure I was going to open my eyes and see him standing there laughing at the foot of my bed. Nope.

There was no one there, but for almost sixty seconds my bed shook. Things were rattling in my room. Then it dawned on me. *Oh, my gosh! It's an earthquake!* But just as I started to panic and jump out of bed it stopped. I laid awake for quite some time waiting for it to happen again. It didn't. After what seemed like forever, I fell back asleep.

The next morning I showered and went down to breakfast. Everyone was quiet and just looked at me. "What?" I asked.

"Oh, nothing." Fred and Jean both answered smiling at each other.

"Did you play another trick on me last night, Fred?" I asked noticing their snickers.

"No, why do you ask?" He grinned looking at Jean.

"Because my bed went thud and then shook for awhile last night and I was sure it was you playing another joke."

Before I could get the entire explanation out the room exploded with laughter. Even Rosa Linda and Isabel roared with laughter.

"What? Did you? But how did you do it?" I asked extremely confused.

Finally, the laughter subsided and Jean offered up an explanation. "No, Joe Lynn, that was a pretty significant tremor. But, as we laid there in bed last night wondering ourselves if it was going to be the 'big one' or not we laughed quietly knowing that you would probably think it was Fred." Jean turned to say something in Spanish to Rosa Linda and Isabel, and once again the room erupted in laughter. Even I joined in this time.

"Yep, that is exactly what I thought. By the way, what is a tremor?"

"A 'tremor' is what we call a minor earthquake around here. But that one last night was pretty significant. It was weird too. It came on with a 'thud' as you called it and then tapered off its trembling."

"Get used to those. We have several of them," Fred said. "It's better than having one great big one that destroys the entire city. They keep calling for a big one around here, but hopefully these little ones will keep the pressure from building and we can avoid a big one."

"Uh, yea, I'm with you. Let's hope the 'big one' never comes." I said. "That one last night was big enough for me."

We all sat down to breakfast and discussed the events of the day and the errands that needed to be done. I knew I needed a trip to the post office to mail my letter back home and to see if I had received any. Receiving cards and letters from friends and family kept me going each day. This was really before e-mail became so popular and besides Retalhuleu would not have Internet service for several more years.

Part of my job the first few months in Guatemala was to go down to the children's day care at the church that the missionaries attended and supported. The day care was a service that the missionaries provided for the local women who had to work to feed their children. Many of the men were drafted into the military, out of the area looking for work, or had moved on to "greener pastures." The mothers had to become maids in order to provide for their families.

So, Fred and Jean paid a couple of ladies in the church to not only "baby-sit" the children, but also teach them and provide them with two hot, nutritious meals. I taught the ladies how to teach, provided them with some curriculum and got to work with the children on hygiene and nutrition. I also taught them English, while they taught me Spanish. In the beginning, my Spanish was not too good, but as the days turned into weeks and the weeks turned into months my Spanish greatly improved.

When I first began going to the day care I was nervous. I was not sure how I was going to communicate. I did not remember much of my Spanish from high school since I had not used it in ten years. I didn't have an interpreter either. However, I learned very quickly that where there is the desire to communicate, there is always a way. It was not long and the ladies, children and I were communicating just fine. I soon started looking forward to visiting the children each day and discovering what interesting thing I was going to encounter from day to day.

Each day the children would try and tell me stories of their lives. Most of them did not have dads, or at least did not know them. A couple of the kids did not have mothers either. Their grandmother, who also worked as a maid each day, raised them. As I listened to their stories by picking up words here and there and splicing together the stories in my head, I also imagined a picture in my mind of how each house must look. Each story conjured up an image in my mind as they told it. It wasn't until one day I had to walk one of the children home to retrieve some much needed medicine that I saw my images were all wrong.

I had imagined their houses based on my experiences in the United States. Even my worse imaginations were tainted by life in America. Suddenly, all my preconceived ideas were gone. Even right there in the midst of Reu, a very large town on the West coast of Guatemala, there was poverty like I had never seen before. Hidden behind a cement wall was another life beyond the one my eyes could see. Life was already quite different on this side of the wall than it is in the States, but this. This was unimaginable for me.

I could tell that the little girl was so proud of her humble abode. I couldn't bring myself to call it a house. It wasn't a house. It was some wood poles, cardboard, banana branches, banana leaves and some twine. Dirt floors. Open fire pit with stones and metal scraps for a stove. Refrigeration was items buried in the dirt to keep them cool. Her "bed" was cardboard laying on the dirt floor in a corner of the area marked as her hut. They apparently just relieved themselves wherever they could find, just feet from their humble abode.

The little girl was so excited to be able to share her home with her new American friend. All I could do was show my excitement for having the opportunity to visit and share a part of her life. I smiled and with all the sincerity that I could muster up said, "¡Qué bueno!" (How nice!) The face staring back, searching my eyes for acceptance simply smiled and motioned for me to follow her back to the center.

My judgment and imagination got an adjustment that day. This all-American girl got a lesson in humility that she never knew she needed. About ten steps outside the cement wall that hid her home, with eyes staring straight ahead, the little girl reached for my hand. She shared her home with me, now she was sharing her heart. There was a bond between us. One only we knew about. That was good enough for her.

Not long after I moved to Reu Fred had to fly back to the States and pick up another vehicle that was being donated to the work in Guatemala along with some needed supplies. Fred was glad that I was there because I could keep Jean and their toddler company. Jean was also pregnant with their second child.

I had pretty much completed my work with the day care teachers and children. I just went every so often to keep in touch with them and assess any new needs or issues. I had moved on to helping Jean with different aspects of the ministry since she was pregnant. From time to time I even helped Fred with the equipment and evangelistic campaigns. I visited a couple of the local orphanages occasionally to see if I could be of assistance in any way.

One evening while Fred was gone Jean and I were watching a movie on one of the English channels on cable. The town cable company had a big satellite dish, and every so often they would turn it so the customers would end up with all different channels. Just when I would learn the channels and schedule it would change. Besides, it wasn't as if I had a lot of time to watch television. Sometimes in the evenings or on the weekends I would get a couple of hours of free time to sit and enjoy some English entertainment.

The movie being played the night Jean and I got the opportunity to watch was called, *Moon Over Parador,* starring Richard Dreyfus. Jean and I laughed from the beginning of the movie to the very end. We swore that it had to be written by Americans who lived in Guatemala. Parador had to be filmed on location in Guatemala. The similarities in the two Central American or South American cities were incredible. Jean and I had found ourselves in a few of the same situations in which Richard Dreyfus found himself. We weren't sure if other Americans found it as funny as we did or if it took living in a Central or South American country to truly appreciate it.

It was also during the time Fred was away in the States that one very mixed up rooster got the best of my very last nerve. I didn't even realize that the neighbor just over the wall outside my room had chickens. It should not have come as a surprise because nearly everyone in Latin America has chickens somewhere on their property. I had gone to bed extremely late that night because Jean and I had taken advantage of the fact that we still had electricity at 10:00 or 11:00 p.m., and stayed up to watch a John Candy movie. We were in desperate need of good, hardy laughter. I had no sooner fallen asleep when I was rudely awakened by a rooster crowing. I thought I had been asleep all night and that it was time to get up, but it was still very dark outside. I glanced at my alarm clock and much to my dismay it was only 2:28 a.m. and I had only been asleep for about an hour.

Why is this rooster crowing in the middle of the night? I thought to myself as I laid there fuming in my bed. I laid awake for hours trying to go back to sleep, but every time I would enter that zone between twilight and oblivion I would be jolted back to the harsh reality that a Guatemalan rooster could not tell time. I would have dreamt of fried chicken all night, but you have to be asleep to dream! By 8:00 a.m. I was so aggravated from "cock crowing sleep deprivation" that when asked what I wanted for breakfast I quickly replied, "Gallo!"

Rosa Linda looked at me rather bewildered, but Jean immediately laughed. She had encountered a few mixed up roosters during her years in Guatemala too. Rosa Linda asked Jean why I was so upset and why I asked for rooster for breakfast. Jean explained. Rosa Linda giggled then handed me my eggs and said in Spanish, "This is as close as I can get to rooster this morning."

"This will do for now," I replied, and gave her a wink of my eye.

The rooster's nightly serenade lasted throughout most of my stay in Guatemala, but finally after a few weeks, maybe months, I got used to it. It was near the end of my year in Reu that I noticed one evening that the neighbor no longer had any winged pets in their yard. Chickens and roosters were nowhere to be found. *Huh. I wonder how long they've been gone?* but quickly moved on to more important thoughts.

A few days later Fred returned from the States with a van that was donated to the ministry. It would really come in handy for transporting people and equipment to the clinic and campaign sites. However, before Fred could actually use the van he would have to travel to Guatemala City to legalize it. Everything had to be registered with the government. In Central America this usually took a few days. So, Fred, Jean and their one-year-old daughter headed for Guatemala City to do paperwork and get away together for a few days. Although I had not been in Guatemala very long and did not speak the language very well, I assured them that I would be fine. After all, I had Rosa Linda during the day and Isabel in the evenings and at night to keep me company and help if I needed anything. As they were getting ready to leave Fred informed me that a pastor would probably stop by and ask for him concerning a meeting they were planning for the next weekend. Jean had given me instructions on some other issues concerning the daycare workers and other household issues. Then as they pulled out of the carport and started to pull away Jean shouted, "Oh, don't forget the trash man comes tomorrow so bring your trash down from upstairs, OK?"

"OK," I shouted back with a "thumbs up" sign.

It was just after noon when they finally pulled away. I had enough letters to write to keep me busy the rest of the day. Rosa Linda had dinner ready by 5:30. She told me the food was ready and explained how to keep the leftovers. Then she said she would see me in the morning as she waved goodbye and walked out the door toward the front gate. I thanked her and wished her a good night.

In that moment, it hit me. *I am all alone in this world. I am in the middle of a foreign country, I do not really speak the language well yet, and I am alone in this big mission house. What would I do if thieves broke in? What if there was an earthquake? What if rebels came and started shooting up the town? Wow! I am really all alone.*

I quickly redirected my thoughts to something more positive. There was nothing I could do if any of those things happened. So why worry about it? I had plenty to do to occupy my mind and time.

That night I enjoyed a quiet little dinner with Isabel of fresh garden salad, BBQ chicken with rice, and fresh brewed iced tea. It was wonderful. Isabel cleared the table while I wrapped up the leftovers, just as Rosa Linda and Jean had taught me, then Isabel and I washed up the dishes together. Afterward, Isabel retired to her room to do homework, shower and then go to bed. She had one more day of school for the week.

I decided to take advantage of the peace and quiet and lack of work to find a nice American show to watch on the only English speaking channel the cable company had on this month. Except for a sports channel that I was just not into. It happened to be an old re-run of "I Love Lucy." About halfway through the episode where Lucy had to pack the chocolate candy into the boxes the lights and TV flickered, the fans slowed down considerably, and after about 3-4 minutes everything went black. *Great! Just when I get the opportunity to watch TV, there's a rolling blackout,"* I thought to myself.

So, I did what most everyone else did in Reu during a blackout, I went to bed! Sometimes when Fred and Jean were home, we would all play Pinochle at a table setup in the courtyard by lantern or candlelight. I didn't know how to play Pinochle when I first arrived in Guatemala, but Jean told me soon after I moved in that if I was going to be a missionary, rule number one was that I had to learn how to play Pinochle. She hoped I would learn it quickly and get to be real good at it. Once a month or so, our missionary friends from the mountains would come down and spend the evening playing Pinochle. They were good and she needed a partner who could help her win on occasion.

Isabel, who was upstairs doing her homework, hollered down and asked if I was all right. "Sí. Estoy bien!" I answered. *Yes. I am fine.* Isabel reminded me not to open the refrigerator or freezer while the power was off. We figured it would be off the rest of the night. So, that night, Isabel and I both took a shower in cold water, in the dark,

81

and then went to be around 9:00 p.m. As I climbed in bed that night I noticed how incredibly dark it was with no lights on anywhere. I laid there in bed for a while thinking of how lonely I was. I am not sure now if I felt so lonely because Fred and Jean were gone, because I was in a foreign country, because the lights were off, or because I really was lonely.

Due to the fact that I went to bed and went to sleep earlier than usual that night I awoke a little before daybreak. The power had come on sometime in the middle of the night and so I jumped up, took a shower and went downstairs to get a glass of orange juice, write another letter, and wait for Rosa Linda to arrive. She began work at 7:00 each week day morning and was off on the weekends to be with her family and tend to her own household. I had just finished my first letter home when I heard the gate squeak open. Shortly thereafter I saw Rosa Linda's smiling face.

"Buenas dias," she said with a big grin from ear to ear.

"Buenas dias, Rosa Linda," I answered back. It truly was a good morning. So far anyhow!

Rosa Linda went to work immediately preparing breakfast for Isabel and me. Isabel was showering and getting dressed for school. This was Friday morning and she had another day of classes before the weekend break. Isabel came from a large family. Her mother was having difficulty caring for her children and sending them to school was out of the question for her. Fred and Jean had taken her under their wing and were paying her way to go to school, get an education and hopefully someday make something of herself. She lived with them during the week and often times would go home for a visit on the weekends.

Soon Rosa Linda was hollering for Isabel to come down to breakfast where the food was laid out on the table. The three of us casually chatted over breakfast. Actually, they chatted and occasionally I would be asked something I could understand and would give them a short reply back in Spanish. I still wasn't able to communicate as well as I would like. I was working on it though and I knew it would happen soon.

After breakfast, Isabel headed to school, Rosa Linda cleaned up the dishes and then she and I sat down to make out the day's list of needed grocery items that she would buy at the market for the rest of the day's meals and all the meals for the weekend while she was off. Soon the list was complete and she headed out the door to market. This usually took an hour or two depending on how many days' meals were being bought. We had to walk several blocks to the open market place, shop from stall to stall to find the freshest food at the best prices. This usually included bartering with the vendors. Some of them, though, were very firm in their prices and would not budge!

As Rosa Linda headed out the door to the market I giggled as I remembered the first time I went to market with her. Jean thought it would be a good way to learn the language, the routine and customs of Guatemala. Oh, I got a lesson that day, but it wasn't in Spanish. It was a lesson in life, death and the pursuit of "fresh chicken!"

As we entered the market area, what a visual and olfactory overload I experienced! My eyes beheld a huge concrete building with a metal roof. Surrounding the building on all sides were trucks, stalls, animals of every kind and people scurrying here and there. I remember as my eyes focused on the site my nose inhaled the most horrendous odor. *What is that horrible smell?* I wondered to myself. Upon closer inspection, which I could have done without, I noticed that there was trash everywhere. Trash of the decaying kind. There was rotting fruits and vegetables, mostly peelings. There was decaying flesh from butchered animals and what appeared to be animal AND HUMAN feces! *Oh, Lord, how do I keep from showing the disgust I was feeling at this moment? How do I keep from offending Rosa Linda or any of these people by the expression on my face?* I just trusted God would help me keep a poker face and hold my breath as long as possible. We were still on the outside; I was praying hard that the inside of that building wasn't worse than the outside! I kept following Rosa Linda as she entered the building and flashed a quick smile as she turned to see if I was still behind her.

As we entered the building I noticed a welcomed drop in temperature. No, it wasn't air conditioned, but it was a cinderblock building that was built halfway underground and was therefore about ten to fifteen degrees cooler than outside. There were also huge ceiling fans everywhere in the building. My senses were on instant overload! I could hardly believe my eyes. There were hundreds of stalls and little shops, which carried basically the same things. You didn't really have a wide variety of items, just a variety of vendors and prices.

Rosa Linda gave me a paper that had the names of a few items that I was supposed to pick up. The first was fresh chicken. It was written in Spanish so I would know how to order it. She pointed me to a vendor and away I went feeling good about my assignment. *This is easy enough.* I thought to myself as I walked toward the lady behind the table. *How hard can this be?*

The lady met my smile with a smile of her own and asked if she could help me. I looked at the words on the paper and said them in my best Spanish pronunciation. It must have been right because she didn't question me or ask me to repeat myself. She immediately said something in Spanish to the man behind me and then asked if there was anything else she could do for me. As I glanced at my paper to see what else was on my list and was answering, no thank you, I heard a loud thump on the table behind me. I jumped and turned around to see what it was. As I turned a man's hand was coming toward my face with a headless chicken in it! He was holding the headless chicken by the feet and handing it to me. I shook my head. NO! That was NOT what I wanted. However, the lady jumped up from the table, grabbed the chicken from the man and handed the bloody thing to me as she repeated the words I had spoken to her…fresh chicken! Yes, I had ordered fresh chicken, but I didn't want it THAT fresh!

I walked back to Rosa Linda carrying the headless chicken by the feet and dripping blood along the way. When she saw me with the item for the evening meal in my hand and the horrified look on my face she doubled over with laughter. She expected it to be wrapped up. They had asked me if I wanted them to wrap it up for me, but I didn't understand what they were asking so I said no. The term "like a chicken with its head cut off" took on a totally different meaning from that day on for me. It took me a few weeks before I volunteered to go to market again. Only after Jean showed me where to go for fresh chicken that had been killed, plucked and cut up did I offer to buy chicken again.

The next morning, as Rosa Linda left for the market, I chuckled to myself as I remembered that first trip with her. I was glad it was her going and not me. I was alone in the house for awhile and I sat down to finish another letter home. After only about two minutes of writing the bell rang at the front gate.

What? Did Rosa Linda forget her key or something? I thought to myself as I laid my pen and paper down and headed to the gate.

I got to the front gate, opened the door and expecting to see Rosa Linda was startled when I gazed into the eyes of a short, scrawny, dirty haired old man who was missing several teeth. He flashed me a wrinkled smile and asked, "Basura?"

Remembering that Fred had said that one of the pastors from the campos would be by looking for him I smiled back at him and said in my best Spanish accent, "El no esta aqui." It means, "He is not here."

The man looked rather puzzled but asked me again a little louder and more pronounced, "Basura?"

OK. Well, I will have to answer him a little louder and more pronounced too. Again I answered, "El no está aqui."

The man shook his head and said, "No. No. BASURA!"

To which I said, "El no está aqui, Señor."

Finally, the pastor must have understood that Fred was not at home and that he would have to come back later because he shook his head and walked away.

I closed the door and headed back into the dining room to finish my letters. I had a smile of satisfaction on my face as I walked back. I had delivered the message that Fred was not there. I had done a good deed. So, I finished my letters, walked to the post office, mailed my letters, picked up new ones and went to a park bench in the middle of Central Square and read them. Sitting in the middle of the park, with the sights, sounds and smells of a foreign country thousands of miles from home, the familiar words of my family suddenly transported me back to my house in Ohio and into the arms of my mom and dad.

Things went just fine the rest of the day. Rosa Linda came home, prepared the vegetables to be eaten, fixed the evening meal and prepared a dish to be placed in the oven for tomorrow's dinner. Isabel came home from school, changed out of her uniform and bounced down the steps to sit in the dining room and chat with Rosa Linda about the day at school while Rosa Linda cleaned up the kitchen. Soon it was time for her to leave for the weekend. She gave us a hug and bid us a wonderful weekend and said she would see us Monday morning. She told Isabel to take the dish out of the oven in fifteen minutes and get the bowl of salad out of the refrigerator. She waved and out the door she went. Isabel had decided to stay with me until Fred and Jean got home so that I did not have to be alone. She had just been home last weekend to see her mom and she could go next weekend too. I enjoyed the company for the night.

The next day a little after noon Fred and Jean and the baby arrived home from the City. I was so excited to see them because I had missed conversation in English. I think I practically attacked them at the door and didn't quit talking until Jean interrupted me with a question.

"Didn't the trash man come by yesterday to pick up the trash?"

"Not that I am aware of." I answered.

"That is strange," she said. "He always comes first thing in the morning."

"Nope. I was here and the only person who came by was the pastor looking for Fred." I said very assuredly.

"What pastor?" Fred asked.

"The one you were telling me about before you left." I answered, wondering how he could so quickly forget what he had told me.

"Joe Lynn," Fred started explaining, "we ran into that pastor on the way out of town and I dealt with him then. There should not have been another one come by here looking for me."

"What did the man say?" Jean asked.

"He just asked for Basura." I answered. "What exactly does that mean anyhow?"

Through uncontrollable laughter Jean finally got out the word, "TRASH!"

So the whole time the trash man was asking for trash, I was telling him that HE was not here!

Days went by quickly and soon it was September and time for my dad's visit. I was excited to see Dad because I missed him. Fred and Jean were excited to see him too because he was bringing a "goody box" or "care package" filled with all the amenities of home. We all had sent our wish list to Mom weeks earlier and now, along with Dad, our goodies were coming. Snickers, Butterfingers, brownie mixes, cake mixes and of course, there was peanut butter and jelly. I had placed boxes of Macaroni and Cheese on the list as well.

We went to Guatemala City to the airport to pick up Dad. It was a good four hour trip one way to the city from Retalhuleo. We decided to take a break from all of the hard work we had been doing and take a small vacation while Dad was visiting. So we took our honored guest to the resort area of Guatemala called Lake Atítlan. Lake Atítlan is the deepest lake in all of Central America. It is a crater lake. It was formed after a massive eruption approximately 86,000 years ago. Since then the caldera has filled with water and three other volcanoes have formed. The largest is called Atítlan. There are two other volcanoes inside the caldera named San Pedro and Tolimán. There are many small towns and villages built around the lake. Most of the inhabitants are indigenous and of Mayan descent. It is rich in beautiful vegetation, flora and fascinating wildlife. The town we were visiting was Panajachel.

Panajachel is the center of tourist trade around Lake Atítlan. Row after row of souvenir shops, which attract tourists from all over the world, line the streets of this beautiful town. There is the business of boating too. Several times a day speed boats would take tourists across the lake to other villages that offered more souvenir shops, restaurants, hotels and of course bars of every size and style. Panajachel had the nicest restaurants and hotels. Each hotel and restaurant had beautifully landscaped gardens, which showcased exotic tropical flowers and plants. Each had fountains and cages that housed various tropical birds or wildlife. It was an awesome place to share memories with my father. Memories that would last a lifetime.

All of the boat trips across the lake had to be taken before 4:00 in the afternoon. We were informed that around that time every day the lake, which was calm and smooth as glass early in the day, would become extremely rough and choppy. It was too dangerous for small boats filled with tourists of all ages to be out on the waters. Many boats had capsized and hundreds of lives were lost down through the years. Now, there was a rule that all tourist boats must be docked by 4:00 each afternoon.

After getting checked in and unpacked, Dad and I took a walk behind the hotel and down to the lake. It was gorgeous. We walked through the garden, and down the sidewalk, lined with beautiful exotic flowers, to the water's edge. We had to keep our shoes on because the beaches surrounding Lake Atítlan were stony. There was no such thing as a smooth, sandy beach. I had on flip flops, so I walked out a foot or so into the lake, which was rather choppy at this point because it was already 5:30 in the afternoon and about to get dark. The water was perfect. Not too cool and not too warm.

Standing on the shore, watching the sun begin to set over the volcanoes, smelling the tropic breeze filled with exotic fragrances, and feeling the warm waters splash over my feet I wished I could stay there forever and imagined that this must be what heaven was going to be like. I had not a care in the world and was content as any young lady could possibly be. The voice of Fred calling us in for dinner interrupted my fantasy and brought me back to reality. It was time to take a drive across town to a wonderful Italian restaurant. Great Italian food in the midst of a tropical paradise? This WAS heaven!

The drive across town to the restaurant was filled with interesting sites. Even after dark, the sights and sounds were enchanting. Latin music interrupted the quiet night and danced its way through the streets, so did a barrage of scents. Cuisines of every kind filtered through the music and filled the air. Flowers gave off their unique aromas as they cooled themselves in the light of the moon. The odors were not all pleasing however. Every once in awhile reality punched us in the nose as we came upon the stench of raw sewage and strong alcohol from a local bar or a passing drunk. Oh, well, it can't all be paradise!

We arrived at the Italian restaurant, which was run by Guatemalans, eagerly walked in and were immediately seated by the hostess. Our server came instantly and took our drink order. I remember what I ordered as if it were today. A watermelon liquado! I loved those drinks. Liquados were made from fresh fruits that were in season and available to the area. You were quite often asked if you wanted it made with milk or water. Milk was not safe if you ordered from street vendors because you never knew if it was pasteurized or not and how long it had been left out in the heat of the sun. If you ordered one made with water you had to ask if they had pure bottled water so that you avoided drinking bacteria and other contaminates.

I preferred my liquado made with water, so I asked the waiter if he had agua pura, *pure water*? The waiter answered that he did and so I looked forward to my cool, refreshing watermelon liquado. That blended fresh watermelon with pure water was a nice treat to my parched tongue. Fred, Jean and Dad all ordered Coke. Coke was the name for all soda pop in Guatemala. Did not matter the brand or the flavor, it was all called COKE. Coca Cola was the national drink of the country, however, so most of the time that is what you were actually served. I am a Diet Pepsi lady myself, so I most often ordered a fruit drink up to and including this trip to Lake Atítlan. Shortly, thereafter I changed to totally bottled Coke or pure water that I drank only from a newly opened bottle that I witnessed them open with my own two eyes.

Approximately ten days after Dad returned home I became sick. I was nauseated one night as I went to bed. Thinking it would pass in the night I went on to sleep and didn't think much about it. Then around 1:00 in the morning I was awakened with severe stomach cramps and diarrhea. The cramps were so bad that I was doubled over in pain. When I wasn't running to the bathroom I would roll around in bed in excruciating pain. I literally felt as though I was going to die. A few hours into the ordeal I even felt that death would be a welcomed relief. I had never in my life felt that way before.

It was sometime around 3:30 am that I cried out for my mother. I am not sure why but I said "Mom" out loud, even though it was barely a whisper. I knew I needed prayer badly and I was in no condition to pray. All I could do was roll around and cry in pain, in between trips to the bathroom. I am not sure how long this lasted or at what time I finally drifted off to sleep, but I awoke sometime after dawn with a high fever and chills. When I did not come down for breakfast Fred came to the bottom of the steps to holler up at me. He asked what I was doing. I could barely get above a whisper and my words were stuttering because my teeth were chattering from the chills. Fred thought that I said I was sleeping, but I said, "I am freezing!"

He said, "Oh, OK," then walked away. Fred was a little hard of hearing and my muffled voice made it difficult to hear. It was a Saturday and we didn't have anything pressing planned right away so I guess he thought he would let me sleep in. However, when lunchtime rolled around and I was still up in my room Jean came up to check on me. By that time I was not chilling, but I still had an elevated temperature. I explained to Jean what happened throughout the night and morning. She was immediately concerned. It could have been a number of diseases. She asked if I thought I could make it down to eat a little soup. I hadn't had anything to eat in 24 hours by then, and I had definitely emptied my entire system of anything I had eaten in the last two days! My stomach was not cramping at the moment so I thought that maybe I would try to eat a little soup. It would not be heavy on my queasy stomach.

As soon as I went downstairs to the dining room the phone rang. It was Mom! She asked me if I was all right. I wondered why she asked me that. She never started our conversation off like that before. Mom always called around bedtime usually. We only got to talk to each other about every other week, but Mom had called last week and was calling me again in the middle of the day.

"Why?" I asked her.

"Because this morning around 4:30 I was awakened by the sound of your voice hollering, 'Mom!' When I realized that you were in Guatemala and not here, I sensed something was wrong with you and I needed to pray. So I did! Now, tell me, what is going on?"

She knew something was wrong and she wanted to know what it was she was praying about.

I began to give her the details of my night and how I had called out for her. We compared the times and with the hour time difference, it was the exact time when I called out for her that she heard me and began to pray. I now know why I was able to drift off to sleep shortly after that. My momma was back home in the States praying!!!

After I hung up with Mom, I had about a half a bowl of chicken soup. It tasted so good, but not twenty minutes later, I was cramping and running to the bathroom. It started all over again. This went on every time I put the least little bit of anything in my stomach. After about a week, Jean had me go to the lab in town and take a specimen. It came back in a couple of hours that I had a severe case of giardiasis! The cure, Jean informed me, was worse than the disease. *Why?* It basically rips out your stomach lining in order to get rid of all the parasites.

Giardiasis is caused by a single celled parasite called giardia lamblia in the small intestines. Its symptoms include nausea & vomiting, watery, foul-smelling stools, severe stomach cramps, and loss of appetite. Many times dehydration becomes a key problem and has to be addressed quickly. I battled with this for four weeks before finally getting rid of it. After a couple more weeks, I eventually regained my strength and the desire to eat again. I became very watchful about drinking water, including bottled water!

After several weeks of hard work on clinics and campaigns, Fred, Jean, their baby and I decided to drive up to the mountain city of Quetzaltenango. It was called Xela by the Guatemalan Indians. So we called it Xela too. It was much easier to say. Xela was an hour drive from Reu straight up a volcano by the name of Santa Rita. The National Geological Society and Central American Volcano authorities say the Santa Rita volcano is about 30,000 years old and is the most active volcano in Guatemala. In 1902, there was a catastrophic eruption that buried several towns and killed at least 5000 people.

In 1922, a secondary dome began to form from the crater in Santa Rita after the eruption collapsed the southwest side. This second lava dome is known as Santiaquito. Santiaquito was very active. It would "pop off," as we called it, at least once a day. Sometimes Rosa Linda would hang laundry on the line to dry and end up having to rewash it due to the layer of fine ash that settled on the clothes throughout the morning from the volcanic ash. We hadn't noticed that it had been several days since it popped off. This daily release of smoke and ash kept the pressure from building and was said to be a good thing.

As we started up the mountain road, which wound around and around the volcano, it became cloudy and started to mist a fine rain. Then it started to snow. *No. Wait. It doesn't snow in Guatemala! So then what is that white stuff?* The road became very slick too. Fred, Jean and I were discussing how strange and dangerous the situation was becoming when suddenly Fred noticed the eerie orange glow above the mountain. Then the white stuff falling from the sky became thick, orange and black. He stopped suddenly and said, "We have to get out of here, quick!"

"Why? What is it?" I asked.

"The volcano has erupted," he replied. "Lava and ash are coming down the side of the mountain."

Fred turned that 4Runner around in the middle of the road. Thankfully there was nothing coming. We slipped all over that road. The ashy mud that was coming down heavily now was making it difficult to see out the window. The wipers couldn't wash it away because the vehicle was out of washer fluid. It was a very bad time to run out. The muddy ash was so heavy Fred stuck his head out the window to be able to see the road.

"I can't see. I can't see anything!" he hollered.

Jean remembered the bottles of pure water she had packed for the baby's formula. So we opened up the bottles and kept passing them to Fred to throw on the windshield so the wipers could wipe away enough ash to see. After what seemed like an eternity, we slipped and slid our way down the mountain and into the town of San Felipe at the bottom where we stopped to wash the windshield. As we looked up toward the volcano we all gasped.

"Oh, dear Jesus!" we said.

The top of the volcano could not be seen. It disappeared in a cloud of ash and smoke. It would be the next morning after the sun came up that we could all see what had happened the day before. One side of the volcano had blown out. Due to the heavy rain during the eruption, a mudslide covered two farming towns on the hillside. We later discovered that twenty three people lost their lives that day. Four hikers from the city of Quetzaltenango or Xela, as we called it, were killed. They were hiking the rim of the volcano when it erupted. Their bodies were recovered the next day. Sadly, Fred and Jean knew the hikers, and the tragedy was made very personal.

The road between Reu and Xela was completely blocked by the initial blast and subsequent landsides. It took over two weeks before the road was cleared enough for traffic to get through. We couldn't get to our friends in Xela and they couldn't get to us.

Things were very quiet as we realized that we all came very close to dying that day. We knew that many had lost their lives, but didn't realize how many until a few days later. If we had not been delayed in leaving Reu due to a flat tire that had to be changed, we would have been right in the midst of the blast. We had renewed appreciation for grace and divine protection, which kept us safe that day.

That wasn't the only brush with death I had that year in Guatemala. One day I was up in my room resting after a long hard morning at the daycare. I had come home and had eaten lunch then excused myself to my room to rest and cool off from the extreme heat and excessive humidity that day. Suddenly, I noticed a burst of cool air rush into my room from outside. *What was that?* I thought to myself. It felt great, but it was very unusual. So I got up from my bed, opened the metal door, and walked out onto the balcony. I noticed that in the last thirty minutes there was what felt like a 20 degree drop in temperature. Maybe more. A strong wind was blowing and was gusting from time to time. Oh my, it did feel great! I turned behind me to the West to see a huge white wall of clouds approaching. It was like nothing I had seen before and I had seen a good many clouds in my 27 years, but nothing like this. Then the rain hit! Fast and furiously. I ran inside. I had to close all of my windows that faced the West. I also had to grab a towel from my bathroom, roll it up and shove it underneath my door. Water was pouring in and flooding my room.

Wow! I hadn't been in anything like this before. There was an enormous amount of wind. Constant strong wind that would gust so powerfully that I was sure it would rip the metal roof right off my room. Then lightning. Flashes and flashes of lightening. It was like the grand finale at a fireworks display. Boom! Thunder so loud it shook the cinderblocks of my room. Suddenly, I heard a faint familiar voice through all the noise. It was Fred.

"Joe Lynn! Are you all right?"

"Yes!" I hollered back.

"You should come down here to the lower level. It is much safer!"

"All right. I'll be right down." I answered.

Why is it safer down there? I thought to myself. But I did as I was told.

98

I opened the metal door to my room and with a rain poncho on I stepped out into the tumultuous storm. I closed the door behind me and took two steps down the stairwell when BOOM! A bolt of lightning struck the metal roof of the room just below me, a mere ten feet away. It was so close I heard it crackling, and felt the hair rise up on my body. It was also so bright that I was blinded for several seconds. I could not hear for a few seconds afterwards from the sound of it. I stood frozen on the steps. It seemed like an eternity. Then, once again, a familiar voice brought me back to my senses.

"Joe Lynn, are you all right?" There was panic and obvious concern in Fred's voice. "Joe Lynn?"

I still stood frozen on the steps. I was soaked, even through the poncho. I tried, but I couldn't move. Then I felt an arm wrap around my shoulders and move me down the steps, across the courtyard and into the safety of the living room where Jean, the baby and Rosa Linda sat gazing at me with searching eyes.

"Are you all right, Joe Lynn?" Jean asked softly.

"Uh, yea, I think so." I paused. "I was nearly struck by lightning!" I said suddenly and with much emotion as the reality of what just happened hit me.

The storm roared on for a few more hours. Wind, stronger than I had ever seen, blew constantly with a roar. Rain came down out of the sky like God was using a water hose. Then, as quickly as it rolled in, it rolled back out. Fred asked if I wanted to go for a drive in the 4Runner to see the storm damage. I was game. So, out we went into the streets of the town and observed the devastation. Wow! I had no idea what happened since we were inside that cinderblock compound, but now being out and about I watched in shock. Complete rows of make shift houses were gone! Water ran in the streets like a raging river. Destruction was everywhere.

Fred broke the silence first. "I didn't want to say anything while it was going on, Joe Lynn, because I didn't want to scare you, but you just experienced your first Guatemalan hurricane!"

"Hurricane?" I shouted. He nodded his head. "That wasn't just my first Guatemalan hurricane. That was my first hurricane ever!" I said in total disbelief.

It was life as usual in Guatemala after that. Life as usual means, never knowing what to expect from day to day! The day could be boring with nothing exciting happening or it could include brushes with death around every corner. Next thing I knew it was November and Jean's family came down from Chicago to visit her for Thanksgiving. Guatemalans did not celebrate Thanksgiving, of course, since that was an American holiday. However, with Jean's family visiting and me spending the year with them we were going to try and have a Thanksgiving meal to celebrate the way we would if we were in the States. That was much easier said than done. Try finding a turkey in Guatemala! We did finally, but it cost much more than we imagined. Oh, and as far as the rest of the traditional Thanksgiving fixings, we finally found some of them in an American food store in Xela. Once again, it cost the first born of each family to obtain such luxury!

Finally the day came and the turkey was placed with loving care in the oven the night before. Our mouths were watering for the taste of an American Thanksgiving meal. Turkey was one of our favorites! The morning of Thanksgiving began with a call from Jean's sister-in-law. The turkey was ruined! What happened? It seemed the oven temperature settings are different in Guatemala than in the States and something about altitude led to the turkey being charcoal by morning. At least we had mashed potatoes and gravy, homemade noodles that I made, corn, cranberries, coleslaw, and by golly a handful of turkey that was salvaged off of the bone deep inside the turkey. The meal was still delicious and the fellowship with family from home was more important than the perfection of the traditional meal. It was a very memorable Thanksgiving for me. I didn't even get homesick because Jean's family made it a very special time.

It was quiet and rather lonely for a few days after Jean's family left but it was soon time for the temporary move to Guatemala City for Jean to have her second child. Not only were we moving to the City for a month or so, but Mom was coming to visit me for my birthday and to bring some Christmas gifts. We would be rather busy for the next couple of weeks and up until time for the baby to be born. I had no idea what was in store for me in the coming weeks.

Finally, moving day arrived. Fred decided that he would take Jean and I and Crystal, their firstborn, on in to Guatemala City and get settled into the apartment while he tied up some loose ends in Reu. We were going to be staying in an apartment at the Wycliffe compound. The Wycliffe Foundation is an organization dedicated to translating the Bible in every language of the world. They have a walled in compound in Guatemala City that is a respite place for their missionaries to come and rest or spend time getting the necessary documentation completed so they can continue their stay in Guatemala. It is a compound of 1 to 3 bedroom apartments, a laundry facility, playground, and gardens within a safe walled-in environment that is guarded by armed guards. This was to be our home for the next four to six weeks while Jean waited for the birth of their next child.

After a week there in Guatemala City, Frank called Jean to have her send me by bus to Reu so that I could drive the truck loaded with needed supplies and follow him in the Jetta back to the city. So, early one morning Jean took me to the bus station, put me on a Galgos (their version of a Greyhound) bus, and waved goodbye as the bus pulled away. Little did I know then how close I would come to never seeing her face again.

I was sitting toward the back of the Galgos over the tire on the right side of the bus as I faced the driver. I sat next to the window. There was someone sitting next to me on the aisle but as the bus pulled away I couldn't tell if they were male, female or what they looked like. I was watching Jean get smaller and smaller as she waved to me until we drove out of sight. I leaned my head against the window, closed my eyes and began to think about everything that needed done back in Reu before we could head back to Jean in the city. I was really hoping that Fred had everything done by the time I arrived so I just had to climb behind the wheel of the truck and follow Fred back to the Wycliffe compound.

Sometime about an hour into the trip I noticed that the bus driver was driving a little fast and sporadic coming down out of the mountains. I had learned that they drive a little crazy in Guatemala from time to time but on these winding, mountain roads in a Calgos bus loaded with passengers was definitely not the time to be driving like Mario Andretti. A couple of times I thought the bus would tip over or go off the side of the mountain. Apparently, so did a few others on the bus because they let out a scream now and then. I began to get concerned and started praying for safety. I started to pray really hard, as the ride became more and more treacherous. This driver just needed to slow down and drive more safely.

It felt like an hour passed but in reality it was just a few minutes when the bus rounded a corner into the town of Esquintla on what seemed like two wheels. The bus driver slammed the bus into a pile of gravel on the side of the road and jumped out quickly. He ran over to a little roadside tienda and grabbed an armful of two liters of Coke. *He just about killed us in order to get a bunch of pop?* I thought to myself. However, as I was thinking this in my head I began to notice that a woman on the side of the road was waving her arms and shouting, "FUEGO! FUEGO!" I recognized that word, but suddenly its meaning escaped me. As I sat there trying to remember what it meant people were jumping up in the bus and scurrying around in a state of pandemonium.

FIRE! Suddenly, I remembered what FUEGO meant. *Fire?* I thought to myself. Just as I remembered what the word meant someone grabbed me and the next thing I know I was standing on the side of the road with the rest of the passengers and bystanders watching flames begin to shoot up from the bus. The driver and some of the men from the bus were grabbing luggage and tossing it from the burning bus. People were pouring bottles of Coke onto the bus trying to put out the flames. I later learned that the brakes had gone out on the bus coming down from the mountains and the driver tried desperately to control it and slow it down until he could safely stop it. By the time we slammed into the pile of gravel in Esquintla the rubber on the tires became so hot that they burst into flames.

It was at that moment that it hit me. I was now almost two hours from Guatemala City where Jean was and over two hours away from Retalhuleu where Fred was. I had no money and spoke very little Spanish. Suddenly, I felt very alone. *Oh, Lord, what do I do? Father, please help me*! I whispered in prayer. I looked up and saw a young man walking toward me. He was tall, thin and had a commanding composure. He reminded me of a soldier. He was looking right at me as he walked toward me.

"You want to go to Retalhuleu?" he asked in Spanish.

"Sí." I replied back.

"Follow me." he responded in Spanish.

So, I followed him. I am not sure why I was following a complete stranger, but I did. What else could I do? We walked over and got in line to get our money back from the driver. Well, half of our money back anyway. After all, he did get us halfway to our destination. He then motioned for me to follow him and we started to walk into town. As I followed this man, I began to wonder within myself. *Where are we going? What am I doing? I don't know this man.* But he just turned around and smiled at me and my fears subsided.

We walked for a few minutes in the hot Guatemalan sun and then walked up to this old wooden building on the opposite side of town. There was a sign that hung lop-sided by one hook above a window with no glass in it. I followed the young man as he walked up to the window. He said a few things in Spanish to the man inside the window, then motioned again for me to follow him. *Sure, why not? I've followed him this far.*

We walked up to a "chicken bus" parked out on the street and he motioned for me to go ahead of him onto the bus. A "chicken bus," as we Americans call them, is an old school bus that has been handed down from the States and equipped with a luggage rack on top. We call them chicken buses because they often have chicken in crates or simply tied together on top. Sometimes, a passenger on the bus might even have several on their lap. They had either just bought them at the market or were getting ready to sell them at the market. Chickens weren't the only livestock found on the bus, however! I had seen pigs and ducks and even goats. There were always twice as many passengers as the limit called for and of course there was no air conditioning. It was hot, crowded and usually very "aromatic" on these buses.

I found an empty seat about halfway back. I sat down next to the window and the man sat down beside me. After several minutes and about sixty more passengers with livestock and produce, we took off down the road. We traveled only about 15 kilometers when we slowed down, stopped and passengers unloaded. The bus driver pulled away again and just a few more kilometers down the road stopped again.

After about thirty minutes it dawned on me that I was sitting on a bus, next to a strange man and not sure where I was really headed. *He could be taking me anywhere. No one would ever know what happened to me.* But just as my thoughts began to run away with me and ignite fear inside, the man laid his hand gently on my shoulder and said, "Esta bien." *It's all right.* As soon as he said those comforting words, the fear left and somehow I knew everything would be all right.

Due to the many stops we made along the way to load and unload passengers and cargo it took four hours to get to Retalhuleu. I was four and a half hours late, but I arrived safe in Reu. As we pulled into the terminal the man got up and motioned for me to get in front of him. *He must be getting off here too.* I thought to myself.

As we inched our way toward the door he asked me in Spanish, "You know where to go from here?"

"Sí," I answered.

I reached the steps of the bus and took one step down to get off when I realized I had not thanked the man for helping me. I turned to tell him thank you, but he was gone! Instead of the young man who had brought me safely to Reu and who had been right behind me, I was looking into the face of a mother and her child. How could he not be there? He was right behind me. I had not gotten off the bus yet. I looked for several minutes for him. I so wanted to tell him thanks. Then I began to realize the details of the last four hours. As I hurried back to the mission house I had several questions that I began to ponder.

How did this stranger know I was headed for Reu? There were many towns along the way and many more after Reu on that route. How did I understand every word he spoke even though he spoke in Spanish? How come he knew when I was afraid even though I never spoke a word of it? Why did the fear leave at the whisper of his voice or the smile upon his face? Finally, how did he disappear when he was right behind me on a crowded bus? Then it hit me. Oh, my gosh, he must have been an angel! God sent me an angel in my time of need. I'm sure he wasn't the first one that God sent me, and I know he definitely wasn't going to be the LAST! Even if he wasn't an actual angel, he was definitely an angel to me!

I ran up the street as fast as I could to the mission home to find Fred. I was already 4 1/2 hours late. It was going to be dark soon and travel in Guatemala at that time was dangerous after dark due to the rebels that were out. When I got to the house I rang the bell and when the door opened one very relieved Rosa Linda greeted me. My very limited Spanish picked up that Fred was out looking for me and was very concerned. She was asking me what happened. Again, to the best of my ability I tried to explain to her in broken Spanish that the bus caught fire and I had to take another slow bus home. That was all I could tell her.

Fred came in within ten minutes and I quickly explained what happened. He was relieved that I was all right, but we had to hurry and take off for the city. It would already be dark before we got there, but we didn't have a choice. He explained to Rosa Linda what I shared with him about the ordeal and then we waved goodbye and told her and Isabel that we would see them in four to six weeks, after the baby was born.

As Fred got in the car and I climbed into the truck, he told me that if I got into trouble to flash my lights at him and he would stop. Those were the days before everyone could afford cell phones and they were virtually unheard of in developing countries. I told him I would and off we went, Fred in front and me closely behind.

All was going well. It was quickly getting dark but we were making good time. We were 2 1/2 hours into the trip and beginning our ascent into the mountains. We were still an hour and a half away when suddenly…pow! The back driver's side tire blew on the truck. I grabbed tightly to the wheel and brought it to a halt on the side of the road.

I quickly flashed my lights at Fred but it was just as he was disappearing around the mountain. I could only hope that he saw the signal before he rounded the curve. I sat on the side of the mountain road with a several hundred-foot drop off on one side and the mountain on the other. Cars, trucks and motorcycles were zooming past me. Many of them too close for comfort. Three and four lanes were many times made out of the two real lanes in Guatemala. *Oh, dear Jesus, what do I do?*

My doors were already locked, but I rolled the windows up as I sat there in the truck waiting for Fred to notice that I was no longer behind him. I prayed that no one else would walk up to the truck. Finally, 10 to 15 minutes later a car pulled up behind me and a man got out and began to walk toward the truck. Oh, thank God, it was Fred!

"What happened?" he asked.

"I had a blow out!"

"Why didn't you flash your lights at me?" he asked with obvious concern.

"I did, but it was just as you were rounding the curve!" I answered with a lump in my throat.

"It's all right." he said consolingly. "At least you are not hurt!"

Fred walked to the back of the truck, examined the situation and began to pull the spare out. "Oh, great! Just great!" I heard him holler with great disgust.

"What?" I asked, but was almost afraid to hear the answer.

"The stupid spare is dry rotted!"

"Oh, my gosh! Now what do we do?" I asked.

"I have to drive 20 minutes back to that last town and see if I can get someone to fix this spare!" he replied. "It's almost 6:00 and most, if not all, of the shops are closed."

"I will get my purse and lock up." I said as I began to walk toward the driver's side.

"No. I'm sorry, JoeLynn, but you are gonna have to stay with the truck!"

"What? Why?" I asked frantically.

"Because the cap on the back doesn't lock and everything we own that is of value is in the back. We would come back to find the truck empty and stripped of its accessories." he explained. "I'm sorry, JoeLynn. I wish there was another way."

I slowly walked back to the truck and climbed inside. He told me to roll the window up and not to let anyone in. Duh! He didn't have to explain that. Only it was dark outside now and still 86 degrees. *Great! By the time he gets back, even if no one gets me, I will have melted into the front seat by then!* I thought to myself. Yep. It was official. I was having a bad day and definitely feeling sorry for myself.

Fred took the spare and headed back into the last town we had passed which was 20 minutes back. He said he would hurry as quickly as he could. I knew that I would be sitting there on the side of the road in the dark for about an hour. After all, twenty minutes there, twenty minutes back and about twenty minutes to fix the tire all added up to an hour. That was if he could even find a place open to have it fixed.

Sure enough, an hour later Fred pulled up, put the spare tire on the truck, and we were ready to roll again. By this time it was now after 10:00 at night and we still had an hour and a half drive into the City. I was more than ready for this day from hell to be over!

We pulled into the Wycliffe compound at midnight. I had left there 16 hours earlier! Jean came running out and asked where we had been and what took us so long. She expected us eight hours ago. There was no way to get in touch with her to let her know what was happening. We sat down together and I gave a detailed account of the entire story with both of them. We all realized how many times I came close to dying that day and how God miraculously delivered me out of every situation.

The year I spent in Guatemala was special training for me. Little did I know then that I was being groomed for the ministry that God was calling me to. I learned so much from Jean that year. I was being prepared for the things that God had in store for me. I would some-day become the nurse that I had always desired to be. I would answer the call to medical missions and travel the world. God placed a love for the Hispanic people in my heart that year that continues to grow ever stronger. I left Guatemala having received more from the people of that country than I could ever have given them.

There is so much more I could share of my year in Guatemala, but there are not enough pages to hold all the memories I have of all that I experienced. That year was just the beginning. A stepping-stone to a new threshold that I was to walk through. A new chapter was about to be written in the book of my life.

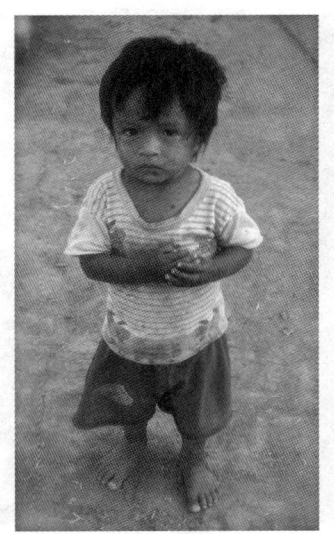
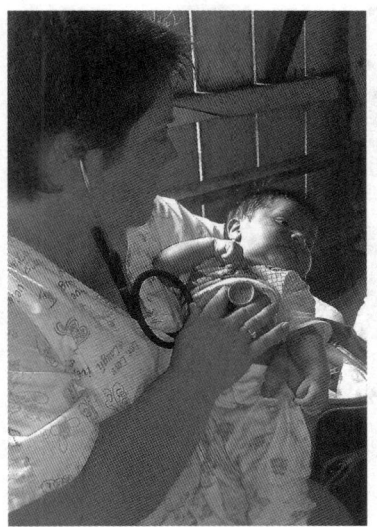

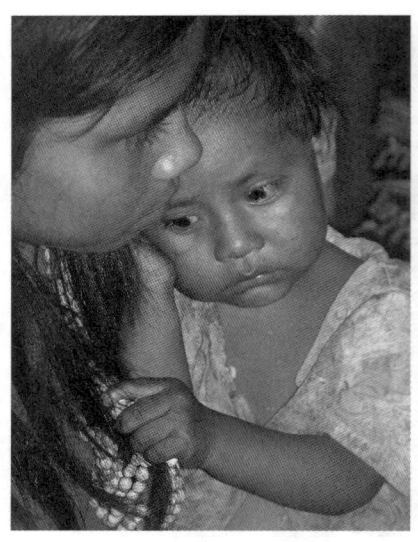

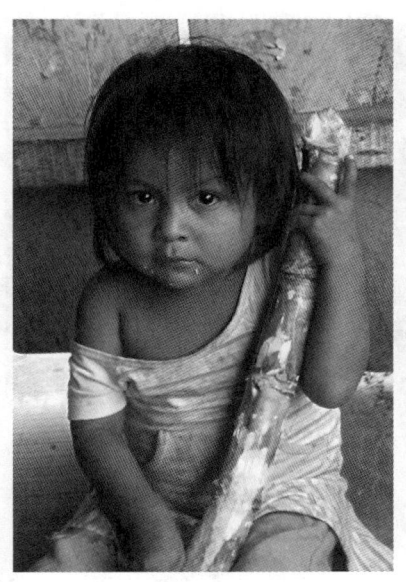

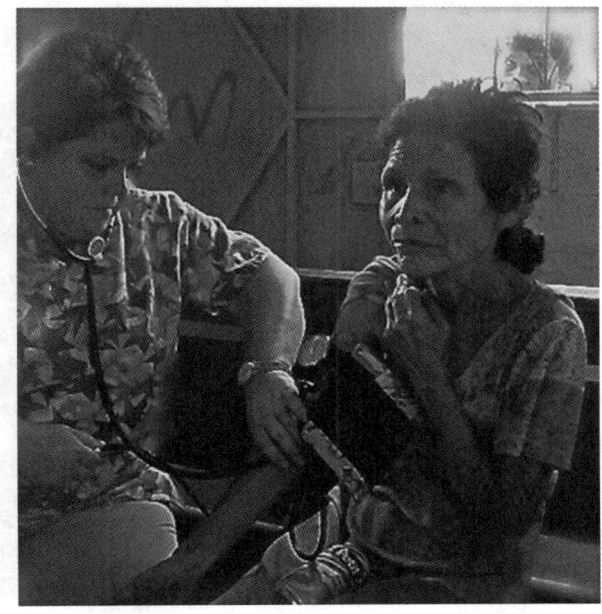

Chapter Four

"Good afternoon, ladies and gentlemen, we will now begin boarding our first class passengers for Continental Airlines flight 419 to Guatemala City." The lady's voice was professional and pleasant. I quickly glanced down at my ticket stub again to confirm my row and seat number as I had done probably twenty times in the previous thirty minutes.

It was my first trip outside the United States since my father's death. After two years of running from the call to missions, and searching for answers to the questions that kept me in my comfort zone here at home, it was time to come face to face with the fear that held me captive.

I was heading back to Guatemala, back to the jungle of the Petén.

"7 F. They gave me a good seat." I thought to myself.

However, there in Houston, waiting for the flight to Guatemala City, the passengers were quite different. Several families looked as though they were returning home to Guatemala after visiting relatives in the States. Most of them were speaking Spanish. I could understand most of what they were saying.

The lady behind the ticket counter made another boarding call. The next announcement would summon the boarding of my row, so I gathered my carry-on and got my boarding pass ready to hand to the lady at the gate. Finally, my row was announced and I made my way to the line.

"Thank you, Miss Daugherty. Have a wonderful flight," the lady said with a smile as she handed me my ticket stub.

As I reached the door of the plane, I paused just outside the doorway. Inside my head there was a battle raging. *Do I really want to do this? Maybe it's still too soon.* I questioned myself.

"Your dad will be home Friday. Are you coming over?" Mom asked over the phone.

"Yes, when will you be back from the airport?" I asked.

"His plane doesn't get in until 6:00 and by the time we stop for dinner and drive home it will be after 10:00."

"Well, I'll stop by on Saturday morning then."

We hung up the phone and I thought about how long it had been since I saw my father last. He was in Guatemala for two months building a home for one of our missionary friends. He was home for three weeks and then left for West Africa. Dad was in Sierra Leone, Liberia, and the Gambia for three months and now he was finally coming home for a while. I knew he had to be tired. He was tired and not feeling well before he left on this last trip to Africa.

Finally, Saturday morning I drove over to Mom and Dad's house to welcome Dad home and hear all about his trip. Dad always had interesting stories to tell after each of his trips. After years of desiring to be a missionary, Dad was finally fulfilling his dream. I was the one who never wanted to be a missionary, and Dad was the one who always wanted to be one. He had been taking trips in and out of Guatemala and Africa for several years now. He was usually a quiet man until he got to talking about his trips. He would then become very dramatic and demonstrative as he recalled the things he saw and experienced.

When I arrived at Mom and Dad's house I found Dad sitting in his lounge chair in the sunroom. He was wrapped up in a blanket. This seemed strange since it was the middle of June. It was an extremely hot day, but Dad was chilled. I went to hug him, but he put up his hand to stop me.

"You better not come too close right now, Sis. I have a cold and I don't want you to take it home to the kids in your daycare." he said with that grin of his. "I will give you a hug later when I'm feeling better."

I sat across the room from him as he told me about some of his encounters in the jungles of Africa. He told of his three days in a village with a tribe and how they took him in as one of their own. He told stories of eating from the "communal pot" with his bare hands, and of being "robed" with the ceremonial robe of the tribe's chief. He was made honorary chief of the tribe. I didn't learn why he was made an honorary chief until a couple of weeks after he died.

It was quite interesting and I sat glued to every word he said. He had a bag of "goodies" from Africa that he wanted me to give to each of the kids in my daycare and to the kids at the church. Then he brought out an African outfit and a doll that he bought which was made by some of the tribal women. He had set it aside especially for me. He showed off some of the musical instruments he picked up over there that he wanted us to learn to play at the church. Oh, yes, and there were a couple of songs he wanted Steve to learn so we could sing them at the church. He was sure that Desireé would be able to pick up on playing the instruments. It was a wonderful afternoon we spent together.

Had I known then that it would be our last father-daughter conversation we would have on this earth, I would have treasured it more and made it last even longer. I would have said the things I wanted to say and done things that I didn't get the chance to do. I'm not sure how, but it just would have been different. Had I known.

Six days later, Dad was gone. He died of malaria. What we all thought was just a cold that he got from sitting under the air conditioner on the plane ride home from the jungles of Africa, turned out to be a deadly strain of malaria. By the time we figured it out and got the medical attention he needed, it was too late. Even the infectious disease doctor from the Center for Disease Control and Prevention (CDC) said that even if we would have known and got him to the hospital sooner, it would have been too late to save him. The disease had infected over 70 percent of his cells by the time he made it home.

My world suddenly changed. I had so many questions. Missions, which had become my passion also, was now a painful consideration. I wanted nothing to do with missions ever again. The call to missions had taken my father from me. At least that was the way it felt at the time. I never wanted to go back to Central America again and I definitely would NEVER go to Africa! I never wanted to leave my country again. I didn't even want to discuss any aspect of missions.

I needed answers. I needed to know what happened to my father and why. I needed assurance that the same thing wouldn't happen to me. Finally, I received the answers to the questions, which kept me from fulfilling the desire of my heart. For the previous two years I had buried the desire and passion for missions deep within me. I knew what I had to do. I had to face the truth: the truth that Dad was gone from this earth and wasn't coming back. He wasn't on an extended mission's trip. He was dead.

I wasn't there when he died. It was a closed casket ceremony. I never visited the grave for two years. It was time to face the facts. I drove to the cemetery. I stood at the foot of Dad's grave staring at the headstone. It was the first time I had seen it. There in big bold letters was his name. Above his name was an open Bible and the last words that he spoke to his mother before he left for Africa, "I must be about my Father's business." She had asked him not to go because she could tell he was tired from the last trip. Those were his last words to her.

Now as I stood at his grave staring at his name, reality stabbed me in the heart. I shed a few tears then whispered through trembling lips, "Good bye Dad. I'll see you soon in heaven, but until then…" I choked on the next few words. "Until then, I will..." Before I could finish what I was saying, I heard these words, "Pick up the torch and finish the race." At that moment, I felt as though someone stood behind me and placed a coat over my shoulders.

Chapter
Five

There were two smiling faces of flight attendants greeting me, so I flashed them a quick smile as I stepped through the door and onto the plane. "Good afternoon," they said at the same time. "Welcome aboard," the older one said with a wink of her eye.

"Thanks," I replied with a forced smile.

I was traveling with a couple from my church. It was their first mission's trip. It was actually the first time that the woman had flown at all. To say the least, it turned out to be an interesting trip for them also.

We found our row, just past the first class section, and I put my belongings under my seat. I don't like to put my things in the overhead compartment because I usually want to use my computer or read a book while I am flying to help pass the time. I don't like to get up and down and bother surrounding passengers, so I just place my belongings under my seat where they can be easily accessed throughout the flight.

The flight from Houston to Guatemala City was the longest portion of the flight, so I could relax and get some rest. After we landed we would still have a few hours to wait in Guatemala City before we hopped a commuter flight to the Petén. I tried to sleep; but it escaped me. I had been preparing myself for that trip for two years, and I felt as though I was ready.

As soon as the in-flight meal was over and everyone settled in for the duration of the flight, I pulled out my laptop computer and began to type up a few notes. Just as I began typing the lady I was traveling with tapped me on the shoulder and said, "Jo, look!" She was pointing out the window.

I glanced out the window and saw the shadow of the plane projected off of a great wall of clouds. The clouds on our right acted like a giant movie screen, as the sun shone on the left reflecting the shadow of the plane. I had never seen anything like it. The image of the plane, cast onto the clouds, was completely encircled by a brilliant rainbow.

I knew that rainbows are refracted light, but I never saw a rainbow colored prism in a perfect circle surround the shadow of a plane 30,000 feet up in the sky. The most amazing part was that it moved with the shadow of the plane projected onto the clouds so that the plane's shadow stayed in the center of the rainbow.

Something inside told me that this rainbow encircling the plane was very significant. As a child, I knew the account in the Bible where a rainbow represented the promise of God that He would never again destroy the earth with water. The rainbow represented His covenant with Noah.

Seeing the rainbow, I felt as though it was God's covenant with us that He was going to watch over and protect us. No matter what happened we were going to be in the very center of His covenant of protection. It might have been a strange concept, but I really believed it was true.

After watching the awesome sight outside my window for a few minutes, I returned to typing with a peaceful smile on my face. The nervous jitters I had earlier were finally gone. I finished typing some notes, put away my laptop computer, and laid my head back to rest for a while before landing. I wasn't sure how long it would be before I got the chance to close my eyes again.

As I closed my eyes, I pondered the significance of the rainbow. It was amazing the peace it brought to my troubled mind. It calmed the fear that would rise up within me from time to time as I contemplated the trip.

As quickly as the rainbow appeared, it disappeared. However, its appearance affected our hearts and minds throughout the rest of the trip in ways we never imagined. We didn't know at the time why the rainbow appeared. The portion of the flight from Columbus, Ohio to Houston was wonderful. The flight from Houston to Guatemala City had been calm. So, why the promise of protection? We would receive the answer to that a number of times before the trip would end.

We stood in line under the "Pasaporte" sign to get our passports and visas stamped. I looked up and saw a sign that read "Aduanas"

and I prayed that we would not be motioned to go there. "Aduanas" is where the customs officials and armed guards search the suspicious luggage. It was not as though we were smuggling contraband, but the entire ordeal makes even a law abiding individual feel like a criminal. The guards make a mess of one's personal belongings, and then push the weary traveler out the door to deal with his or her opened, discombobulated suitcase as he or she exits the building.

Don't make eye contact, I thought to myself as we headed toward the exit.

We moved slowly closer to the exit. We had to walk past some officials who were doing some last minute searches on visitors before they left the airport. I was shaking inside, but tried to act nonchalant on the outside. Just a few more steps and...

"Señorita," someone said as they grabbed my arm. "Por favor," he said as he pointed to my luggage.

Oh, dear God! No. I knew what was coming. I had been in this situation before.

The ordeal was soon over. It wasn't too bad this time. They just looked in one of the bags, shook a couple of the other ones, and then motioned for us to leave. So, once again we had to gather up our belongings, place them back in the suitcases and make our way to the throng outside.

It was prearranged by the missionaries to have a Guatemalan friend, who lived in the city to meet us at the airport, take us to lunch and then take us back to the airport in time for our commuter flight to the Petén. So, we placed our luggage in lockers at the airport and went with Raúl to a steak house. In the capitol city one can get just about anything, including American foods.

We had a leisurely lunch with Raúl and enjoyed his company for a few hours and then headed back to the airport to make our connecting flight. After gathering up our luggage again we headed to the gate of Aviateca. That is the name of the Guatemalan airlines we were flying to the Petén. It was a small plane, but it looked fairly new and in good shape. At least we weren't flying TACA, which many Americans say stands for "Take A Chance Airlines."

We boarded the plane and sat back for a short thirty-minute flight. Darkness had already fallen. Just a thin pale pink line was all that was left to the sunset. All was beautiful and calm in the city and we had no reason to believe that the flight would be any different.

The main cabin door was closed, the pilot pulled away from the gate and began taxiing down the runway. We noticed that the three of us were the only Americans on the plane. I giggled. I have been the only American on different modes of transportation many times before. Why should this be any different? At least I wasn't all alone this time. We took off without a glitch. San Benito, here we come!

About ten minutes into the flight the skies grew tempestuous and we could see lightning in the distance. Suddenly, the plane began to shake and lightning began to strike all around us. We were flying into a violent storm. For the next twenty minutes we shook and bounced all over the sky. Several of the people on the plane were crying, or screaming. I admit fear had gripped me too. I was praying really hard under my breath. I didn't want to appear frightened to my companions.

Then I noticed the lady with me was crying. She suddenly said, "Jo, I am so scared. Please pray!"

I started to tell her that I already was praying, but before I could get it out, these words came out of my mouth instead, "Remember the rainbow!"

Suddenly, my body relaxed. I realized all fear had gone. I noticed that the lady quit crying and calmed down. We began to recall the rainbow and discussed what it meant. We were calm and peaceful for the rest of the flight and landed safely in San Benito. Although the storm never subsided, our fear did. Regardless of the storm, we were calm and protected. I thought to myself, *so that is why the rainbow.* That was only the beginning!

Our accommodations were a welcomed sight. After the kind of flight we had at the end of an extremely long day, we were ready to call it quits and start fresh tomorrow. The missionaries we were staying with in San Benito had a two-bedroom "house" next door to the local radio station. On the other side of them was the office of the local United Nations Organization. Above the UN office were two small apartments. The smaller of the two apartments was directly over the other. I stayed in the mid-size apartment and the couple traveling with me stayed upstairs in the smaller one.

The first day of our stay in San Benito, which is in the heart of the Petén was a bright and beautiful one. There was no evidence of the storm the night before except for small puddles here and there. I came down to breakfast humming "There's Got to be a Morning

After" and thinking to myself, "*So far this day is off to a good start. Ok, so, I just got up.*"

The smell of breakfast cooking in the kitchen of the main house was very appealing. The missionary's wife is an excellent cook. Actually, so is the missionary himself. He is an Italian from my home state of Ohio. I met him and his wife several years ago on my first trip to Guatemala. I happened to have met several interesting people on that first trip. People that would become my support system later and would often be there when I needed them most.

The missionaries had a full ten days planned for us. We would be visiting villages that were extremely poor and sick. We held clinics in an area called El Mundo Perdido, *the Lost World*. It was way out of town and in a very dense area of the Petén. I worked in the pharmacy with Dorothy and the couple that came with me worked with the dentist who helped us in the clinic. Tom, the missionary, worked one of the medical stations himself. One of his patients complained about her ear. After examining the ear, Tom discovered the problem. He pulled a tick out! We saw over three hundred patients that day. It was an awesome clinic. There was another couple from the United States visiting the missionaries at the same time we were there. I had met them before in Quetzaltenango. They, too, were missionaries when I met them, but had to leave the field due to sickness. They were a wonderful couple and it was so great to see them again. It was like a little family reunion.

On the way home, the ladies rode in one vehicle and the men rode in another. As we bumped and rattled our way home on all of the dirt roads that had been nearly wiped out by the rains we talked about how desperately we all had to relieve our bladders. We were laughing and making jokes about it as we came into the outskirts of San Benito.

Suddenly, Dorothy, said, "See that person there with the bald head walking along the road to the right of us?"

"Yes," we all answered.

"She is the local witch doctor," she said as she turned her head toward the lady and their eyes met.

"SHE?" I asked.

"Yes, it is a woman!" she said and then suddenly grabbed her head.

"Dorothy, are you all right?" we all asked.

As we made the five-minute drive back to the mission home the pain in Dorothy's head got worse. We helped her into the house and took her into her bedroom to lie down. Within minutes she was delirious with fever and head pain. She was rolling around in the bed and moaning with pain. We all walked the house praying and wondering what to do. We prayed. We walked the floors and prayed really hard for about an hour. Then, as quickly as it came on, the pain, fever and delirium left. She was just fine. Prayer and faith in the Name of Jesus can work miracles!

We went to other villages that week and passed out clothes and shoes. In one village we went to the local pastor of the village church invited us to his hut to see his new baby. It was a healthy, beautiful boy. He was so proud! It was his fourth child. The women in our group took turns holding the new little blessing.

After several hours of passing out clothes and shoes and holding a clinic our bladders were full once again. The men, of course, had no problems with that issue. It was easy for them just to relieve themselves behind a tree or bush. Ladies have different plumbing that made it a bit more difficult. We are more modest too, of course. So the pastor informed us that he had an outhouse that the women could use.

Just like in the States, ladies never go to the "powder room" alone. All four of us ladies, the missionary's granddaughter and the pastor's two little girls walked the path to the outhouse to relieve ourselves of our full and now painful bladders. When we arrived we found a small cinderblock room just large enough for a two-hole toilet. The toilet was made of wood just like the ones in the States. First, Marge went in. She was the visiting missionary from the States. She pulled the curtain to the doorway back and walked in. She was prepared. She had her handful of toilet paper she had brought with her from the mission home. She had no sooner walked in when Dorothy began to tell her…

"Oh, make sure you lift the toilet seat and …" Before she could finish her sentence a blood curdling scream could be heard for miles. Out runs Marge pulling her pants up as she ran. Dorothy immediately started laughing. I snapped a picture just as she ran out of the building. The look on her face was priceless! The lady with me started screaming too.

"What's the matter? What happened? What is it?"

However, before she could reply the answer came flying out after her. Bugs! Bugs of all kinds! Mostly flies, but there was also mosquitoes, moths, gnats and other flying insects that I didn't recognize. The instructions Dorothy was trying to tell her was to lift the seat cover and step back until all of the bugs flew out of the hole. Marge didn't get those instructions in time! She lifted the lid as she was sitting down on the seat. As she did hundreds of insects flew out and hit her in the…well, you know! Up off the commode she came, pulling up her pants as she ran out the door screaming! We laughed about that for a long time. And I just so happened to catch it on film. Yes, it is now a "Kodak Moment!"

"Next!" hollered Dorothy.

"Not me!" I said. "I don't have to go anymore!" With that we all laughed again as we walked back to the pastor's hut.

One of the highlights of the trip came on the second to the last day there. We were taken to the ancient Mayan ruins by the missionary. It was only a 45 minute drive to the ruins of Tikal. We could see the tops of the temples sticking up out of the jungle for miles before we reached the entrance to the ancient city. Just inside the entrance was a restaurant, restrooms and a souvenir shop. Between several trees and some thick brush was a narrow path through the jungle that visitors must hike through before reaching the city. It was at least a mile from the parking lot and facilities. The temples could not be seen from the path because the jungle was so thick. The trees and foliage were so dense you could not see the sky in many places.

We began our hike through the forest not knowing what we would see when we finally got to the clearing. It was hot and sticky and wet. Then again, this was Central America. This was the jungle!

Our ears heard many different animal sounds for the first time. Animals we don't have the opportunity to hear in the States. We really didn't see any of them, but we heard them. We did see an occasional bird fly over to squawk at us from high above our heads. We also came upon a monkey here and there. They made big noises for such small animals. Then at one point I thought it was raining. I felt a few sprinkles. I even made the comment that I thought it was raining.

"That's not rain!" the missionary told me without stopping or turning around.

"Then what is it?"

"You don't want to know!"

"Why not?"

"I'll tell you if you really want to know," he said turning to give me an ornery grin.

"Go ahead. You might as well. I pretty much get the picture that it is disgusting whatever it is."

"Monkey pee!" he said without stopping.

"Uh! That is disgusting! Why did they pee on me?"

"They must like you!" he said laughing. "That is how they mark their territory. Some male monkey just laid claim to you."

"Ha ha! Very funny!" He was actually telling the truth, but was enjoying it a little too much. At the time I was rather disgusted by it.

Suddenly, the narrow path opened up like a curtain being pulled back. In the clearing were four large stone temples. They were quite ominous looking. Each one faced another temple at the opposite end of the clearing. They were pyramids. Large circular stones with ornate carvings lined the front of each temple. I noticed each stone was stained the same. It was a strange color that was not found on any of the stones in the temple. There was no particular pattern to the stains and they were on the top and sides of the stones. Tom noticed my intense inspection of the rust colored stains and enlightened me. They were blood stains.

"Blood? Why bl-uh! Oh! Sacrifices?" I asked.

Tom nodded, pursed his lips together and walked on leaving me to ponder what I was observing.

Years, if not decades or centuries, of sacrifices took place on those stones. Sacrifices to the Mayan gods to whom the temples were built. There were signs of sacrifices everywhere. No one really knows what happened to the Mayan civilization. There was evidence everywhere that they were very intelligent, religious, but also war minded. They were extremely aggressive and blood thirsty. They warred amongst themselves often. There are many theories.

This community alone had a large population and yet what happened to them. Where did they go? Did they leave? Were they taken captive? No one really knows. The demise of these people still remains a mystery.

Many of the temples were open to the public to climb to the top. Temple Twelve was the highest temple and the top of it broke through the canopy of trees and towered high above the ceiling of the jungle. From the top you could see for miles and view all of the other temples that barely made it past the jungle ceiling. It was from the vantage point atop Temple Twelve that a scene from Star Wars was filmed. Being the Star Wars fan that I am I recognized it immediately. Of course being the amateur photographer that I had imagined myself being I captured yet another Kodak moment. I had to take this shot back to the rest of my fellow Star Wars fans.

It was on my climb up to the top of Temple Twelve that I received my one and only mosquito bite of the entire trip. I was usually eaten alive on these trips. However, since this was my first trip after my father died of malaria, I went prepared. I had mosquito repellant and I took Skin-So-Soft body oil by Avon. I had heard from someone that it was good for repelling mosquitoes and I was willing to try anything.

I also had a prayer cloth that I kept on me at all times except, of course, when I was in the shower. As I made my way up the wooden steps through the trees surrounding Temple Twelve I noticed a mosquito flying around me. I began to talk out loud to it.

"If you know what's good for you, you will keep on flying!" I said through clenched teeth and pursed lips.

Well, it didn't heed my advice. "Oh, no, you didn't just land on me and oh, you jerk!" I said smacking it until it was just a blood stain with tiny black particles on my hand. "You bite me, you pay the price!"

I stopped, pulled my prayer cloth out and put it on the bite on my hand. I prayed a brief prayer and when I removed the cloth I couldn't even tell where the bite was. I thanked God and went on climbing. I realized as I finished my ascent through the trees to the peak of the temple that instead of being afraid of the bite, I was furious! Nevertheless, the prayer cloth and my prayer worked and there was no sign of the bite. Malaria was not even a consideration. I could not allow it to be a part of my thoughts at that time.

The rest of the trek through the jungle and the Mayan ruins I never received another bite. One bite in ten days in the Guatemalan rain forest is pretty amazing! Especially for me! Jeff, however, didn't fare so well. He received 26 bites just that one day and they became infected. He and Cheryl were visibly worried. I knew they were getting into fear and we had already seen what that could do. So I told them that I would go next door to the radio station and use their phone to call back to the States and ask Mom what to do. She was a mighty prayer warrior and our pastor!

It took me a few times to get through on my calling card. After all, this was Central America and we were on the fringe of the rainforest! Finally, I got through and I related the events of the day to Mom and told her about the mosquito bites.

"What about YOU?" Mom asked quickly. "Did you get any?"

I shared with her the battle with the one mosquito and told her what I had done with the "hanky." She then explained to me that was exactly what the "hanky" was for. She had prayed over it for more than two weeks specifically for protection against mosquito bites and malaria. She lost her husband, but she was NOT going to lose her daughter. She then said that I was to share my cloth with Jeff.

I went back to the apartment and relayed the message from Pastor and I gave the "hanky" to Cheryl to rub on Jeff's bites. Although he suffered from the itching overnight the infection was gone by morning and in a few days the bites were gone too. Thank God he never got malaria. Yes, in the area we visited in the Petén, malaria was endemic. There were many around us who had it. Even the missionary himself had it, but it was being treated and well under control.

The day before our departure we received word that there was a hurricane headed our way. It was going to hit us head on late the next day. The very day we were to fly out. Not to worry though, our flights were first thing in the morning. We could beat it out. Immediately, the radio station next door began disassembling their communications tower. The town's people were scurrying around trying to hurricane proof their properties. We were busy packing and preparing to "get out of Dodge!"

Very early the next morning, before daylight, we brought our luggage down and loaded it up in the back of Tom's little Toyota truck. We went inside to say goodbye to Dorothy and then headed out of town to the airport.

The airport was extremely small there in the Petén. It looked more like a big hanger than an airport. It did have a small tower though. As we drove the twenty minutes to the airport the sun began to rise. It was a clear day! It showed no signs whatsoever that a deadly hurricane was making its way toward us leaving devastation in its wake.

We pulled in, unloaded our luggage and headed toward the ticket counter. It was almost 7:00 am and our plane departed in an hour. No one was at the airport but the four of us and a few employees. We approached the man at the counter, wished him a "buenas dias" and handed him our tickets.

"I'm sorry, but the flight has been cancelled." he said in Spanish.

"Excuse me? Why?" asked Tom.

"Because there is a hurricane coming." he answered.

"Well, it isn't here now. Look outside. It is bright and sunny and not a cloud in the sky."

"Sorry. The 8:00 flight has been cancelled. However, we do have another flight leaving at noon. Would you like it?" he asked nonchalantly.

"We will miss our connecting flight to Houston if we don't get to Guatemala City before 10:30 am." I said.

"Sorry, that is all we have. All flights have been cancelled until Tuesday. It is the noon flight or nothing until Tuesday."

"I don't understand. You cancelled this morning's flight because of the approaching hurricane, but you have another flight four hours later when the hurricane is closer that you are going to keep?" Tom stated rather bumfuzzled.

"That's just the way it is, Sir. Would you like the flight or not? If so, I will have to change your tickets now."

"Yes, we'll take them. What choice do we have?" I answered looking at Tom.

"Are you sure? What happens when you get to the City? What if you can't get another flight out of the City?"

"We'll have to cross that bridge when we get there." I said. "Hopefully, that won't be the case."

We told the ticket agent we would take them and discussed how we needed to stop by the travel agency in town to see about connecting flights to Houston from Guatemala City.

Once we reloaded our luggage and got back into the truck Tom looked at me and said, "Here in the Petén, when the going gets tough, the tough go to breakfast!" We laughed.

"Besides, it is still too early for the travel agency. We can stop there on our way back into town. There is this nice restaurant on the lake that I'd like to take you to."

"Sounds good to us, Tom."

Tom called Dorothy to fill her in on the details of our situation as we headed to the other side of town. We got to Lake Petén and saw this island in the middle of it. There was one way onto it and one way off. A two-mile long land bridge. We started across this two lane land bridge and then realized how narrow the road was. It was beautiful though. It was actually a splendid morning and the lake was lovely, too. The morning sun reflected off the calm waters in golden sparkles. It was hard to imagine at this point what was coming.

There was a little town built on this island. The entire town was built for tourism. In the center of the island was this restaurant called Las Puertas, which means "the Doors." It was called this because all around this restaurant were doors. Doors on three sides. When we got there all of the doors were standing wide open. It was like eating outside except for the roof over our heads. It was really quite charming.

I ordered scrambled eggs and chorizo with a side of frijoles and tortillas. That was a "typical" Guatemalan breakfast and I loved it. We all ordered our food and began talking about rough plane rides and plane crashes. It actually was not a very smart thing to talk about when we were getting ready to fly, possibly under rough weather conditions. I'm not quite sure, but I think Tom started the conversation.

Our breakfast came and it was delicious. Tom and I reminisced about the days in Xela and Reu a few years earlier. We talked about my father since Tom knew Dad too. We talked about all the people we knew and had worked with over the years there in Guatemala and how time changed so many things. We were finishing up our meal and paying the bill when suddenly all of the doors slammed shut! It made us all jump. Then the doors started blowing open and closed. The employees and customers alike started running to the doors to latch them before they blew off. The four of us looked at each other and then Tom finally said, "I think we better get off this island immediately!"

"Good idea!" I interjected.

When we stepped out of the building the sight we saw was shocking. The blue skies were suddenly replaced with black. There was a definite line of demarcation in the sky. The golden, burnt orange sky was being chased away by a wall of ominous black clouds. As the bubbling black wall of clouds approached, the wind picked up. We hurried to the truck and headed off the island across the land bridge. I glanced out the window and noticed how high the waves were on the lake. The calm waters of Lake Petén that previously reflected the golden sunlight like glass was now churning and spewing out angry waves. About halfway across the bridge the waves started splashing up over the road. The little pickup truck was getting to be hard for Tom to handle.

"Uh, now would be a good time to pray! 'Peace, be still' would be nice!" Tom said.

"Seriously!" I said.

After making it across the bridge and back into town, we headed straight for the travel agency to see what the current status was. It was not good!

"No flights out of here until Tuesday, except for the noon flight and that may or may not get cancelled." The travel agent said. She was a nice lady and she tried everything to help us. It was Friday morning and there was nothing else till Tuesday.

"Once you get to Guatemala City there are no flights out to Houston. You will have to stay there until Tuesday anyways." She added.

"You might as well stay here with us and ride this out." Tom suggested.

"I have to work Monday!" Jeff quickly responded.

"Me too!" added Cheryl.

"And I have six children coming to my daycare!" I interjected. "I know we need to get home!"

Tension was getting high. There wasn't anything to do, but stay there until Tuesday or fly to the City and see what we could do from there. There was always the possibility we would get stuck there. We didn't have any money to get a hotel and sleeping at the airport for four days was out of the question!

"Let's just head back to the house and discuss our options there." Tom suggested.

"Sure. That sounds good." I replied.

We no sooner got to the truck than it started raining. The wind and rain were picking up. Our luggage was in the back of the pickup truck getting soaked. It was a good thing that we were only a few blocks from the missionary's home and that they had a carport to keep the luggage out of the rain.

Once inside, the tension really escalated. The missionaries suggested that we just "hunker down" with them and ride it out. Jeff and Cheryl were missing their granddaughter and really needed to get to work Monday. However, if we needed to stay then we needed to stay, but how were they going to reach their family to tell them not to drive two hours to pick us up tonight?

"Look, I'm getting out of here today. One way or another, with or without you. I am getting home tonight." I said very matter-offactly. "I will not accept anything else." I'm not sure why I said that. I was determined to get home tonight. I didn't want to ride out the storm there. I wanted to be safe at home.

"Look, I know you are a faith person and you believe in the power of positive thinking and positive speaking, but I think you need to be realistic. This situation looks pretty impossible." Tom said kindly but firmly.

"I'm calling Mom." I said.

"How?" Tom asked. "It's hard enough to get a call through when the tower is up. Now that it is down, and the weather is terrible, it will be impossible."

"Then pray for a miracle! I need to talk to Mom. She will know what to do!"

With that I walked out the door and inched my way next door to the radio station through the wind and rain and asked to use the phone. They said I could try but that it had not been working all morning.

"God, please let me get through to Mom! I really need to talk to her. She will know what to do." I prayed to myself as I dialed the eleven numbers to get through to Mom's house. I was not even sure where she would be at that moment.

"Hello?" It was Mom! She answered on the second ring. It was truly a miracle. We had better reception with no tower and in the middle of a storm than we did in perfect weather with the tower up!

I explained to Mom what our situation was. Then I asked her what we should do. She asked me what I felt in my heart. I told her I felt we should get to Guatemala City and believe God to get a ticket out to the States. She agreed.

"You will be home tonight!" she said.

That was all I needed! I told her I loved her, hung up the phone, and walked back to the mission home. I told them what Mom had said.

"You mean you actually got through?" they asked.

"Yes, on the second ring of the first try!" I replied.

"Wow, that was a miracle!" Tom said.

"So, what did she say?" Cheryl asked.

"She said we are to get to Guatemala City and God will get us home from there tonight!" I answered confidently.

"Well, OK, if that is what you all think is the right thing to do," Tom said.

"I do," I answered. "I really do."

"Well, I think we should all join hands and pray before we do anything else," Dorothy interjected. "We really need to pray."

"That is a really good idea," I added.

So we all gathered in a circle, Jeff, Cheryl, Dorothy, Tom and I and we began to pray for God's guidance and divine intervention.

We had not been praying for five minutes when Tom's cell, which was laying on the couch where we were standing, began to ring. Yes, the cellular towers were down in preparation for the storm, the wind and rain were kicking up outside as Hurricane Mitch was approaching quickly and yet his cell phone rang.

We stopped praying and Tom answered the phone.

"If you want to get to Houston, get to the airport now," said the male voice on the other end of the phone.

"Excuse me? Who is this?" Tom asked.

"If you want to get to Houston get to the airport now," the male voice on the other end of the phone repeated and then hung up.

"Who was it?" Dorothy asked.

"I have no idea." Tom answered. "I think maybe the guy from the airport." He then shared with us what the voice had said.

"So, hurry and get your things together and we will head over to the airport really quickly." Tom said as he was gathering up some pieces of luggage.

"I don't feel right about this, Tom. Something just doesn't sound right," Dorothy said. "I think you should stop by the travel agent's office and see if they are the ones who called or not."

"All right. I will," answered Tom.

So, we gathered our luggage again and headed out the door to drive to the airport. The rain was coming down pretty steadily. We drove into town through streets that looked more like small rivers than roads.

"Uh, wasn't that the travel agency we just passed?" I asked Tom.

"Yea, but we really don't have time to stop there. The caller said to get to the airport right away," he answered.

"But Dorothy said.."

"I know, but let's just get to the airport and then we can determine what's going on from there," he quickly interrupted.

"Ok," I said and glanced out the window.

There was a Galgos bus getting ready to pull out of the Shell gas station that we just passed. I didn't notice any passengers on it. It pulled onto the highway right behind us. We drove another three or four miles and then Tom turned the signal on to turn left into the airport. We slowed down and Tom began to make the left turn into the parking lot. Suddenly, out of the corner of my eye something caught my attention. I looked up to see the Galgos bus coming straight at us. We were crossway in the road making the left turn. As I looked into the eyes of the bus driver glaring at me intent on hitting us, all I had time to get out was "JESUS!" As I hollered out the Name, Tom shoved the accelerator to the floor.

The sound of metal slamming together and Cheryl's scream rang through my ears. We began to spin around a couple of times and then come to a stop on the side of the road. It all seemed to happen in slow motion. Because Tom hit the accelerator the bus just about took off the tail bed sending our luggage flying into the air before being strewn all over the side of the road.

"Is everyone all right?" Tom asked as he turned around to look back at Cheryl and I in the back seat. His face was white as a sheet.

"Yes, thank you, Jesus!" I answered.

"Yes, I am ok," answered Cheryl.

We slowly got out of the truck as the driver approached, angry as a hornet. I know I saw the Devil in his eyes as I looked up at him before the impact. The driver passed us on the left instead of the right as we turned into the airport. He had his fists clenched on the steering wheel and he had an ugly, snarl on his face when he hit us. He was supposed to pass us on the right and he would not have hit us. I know to this day that he intentionally hit us. He started hollering in Spanish before he ever reached us.

Tom turned to me and said, "JoeLynn, you and Cheryl quickly go on into the ticket counter and get checked in. You speak enough Spanish that I'm sure you'll be ok. I may be awhile here with this, but I don't want you to miss the flight. Jeff and I will gather up the luggage and bring it in as soon as we can."

"OK." I said reluctantly. I wasn't so sure things were going to go very well with this driver.

Cheryl and I walked on up to the door of the airport. A crowd had begun to gather around. There were plenty of "eyewitnesses." As we got to the ticket counter the same man was there from a couple hours earlier. He looked at me puzzled.

"Back already?" he asked.

"Yes, you called and said that we were to get to the airport right away in order to make our flight to Houston."

"No, I did not! There is no other flight." he said emphatically. "I told you there is only one flight out of here until Tuesday and that is at 12:00."

"But someone called and said that if we wanted to get to Houston tonight, be at the airport immediately!" I rebutted.

"Well, Ma'am, it wasn't me!"

"Ok. Thank you anyways." I said with a forced smile.

"That doesn't make any sense." I muttered to myself as I turned facing Cheryl.

"What are we going to do?" asked Cheryl.

"Nothing we can do except sit here and wait for the guys to get finished and get here." With that we found a seat and sat down to wait on the guys. There were a few more people milling around the airport at this time.

About fifteen minutes later, Tom and Jeff came in carrying our luggage. Surprisingly, none of the luggage was damaged. They looked a little ruffled and were soaking wet, but managed to flash a slight smiles as they approached.

"Well, did you get checked in?" Tom asked.

"Checked in to what?" I replied. "There is no flight to check into."

"What?" Tom practically shouted. Then he turned and walked up to the man at the ticket counter. By this time, I am sure that the ticket agent was extremely frustrated with us and just wanted to put us on any plane and fly us out of his airport. Tom talked with him for just a few minutes and actually had the man laughing as he turned to come back to us.

"Well, all I have to say is the Devil apparently makes phone calls and he knows our number." Tom said looking at each one of us. "There is no other explanation. No one here made that call. No one at the travel agency made the call. Furthermore, who else except this man and our travel agent, who is a woman, knows that you are trying to get to Houston tonight?"

"Yes, and I was just sitting here thinking, Tom, that if we had stopped at the travel agency like Dorothy had told us to we would not have been anywhere near that Galgos. You know he purposely hit us. I believe he was trying to kill us!" I said emphatically.

"I know you are right about stopping at the agency, but are you positive about the bus driver?" he asked very seriously.

"As sure as I know my name," I replied.

"How's that?"

"Tom, when I looked up just before he hit us he was glaring at me with a devilish look in his eyes and the steering wheel gripped hard, leaning over it. I know he meant to hit us. Besides every idiot knows you don't pass on the left when the vehicle in front of you is turning left! I am positive he meant to kill us."

"You are probably right!" he said hesitantly. "He was sure mad as a hornet when he got to us. What's more is that I got the ticket and have to pay $1000 to the bus company to repair the fender and my truck is totaled!"

"What? You've got to be kidding! Why? It was HIS fault!" I shouted.

"This is Guatemala, JoeLynn. You know that anything and everything involving a gringo is the gringo's fault. I'm just thankful that they didn't throw me in jail." he replied.

"Yeah, you're right. I remember. Well, we can at least be thankful that none of us were hurt, much less killed!"

"Amen!" they all said in unison.

We only had a couple of hours to wait before the flight took off so we waited there at the airport. We didn't really have much choice since the truck was totaled. Tom called Dorothy to tell her what happened and to let her know that everyone was all right. She was going to have to come out in the rain and pick him up and call for a tow truck.

Within the hour, the twin-engine prop plane landed on the runway and taxied to the tarmac. It didn't even try to get close to the hanger. It just sat out on the tarmac. The proper services were done on it and finally the boarding call was given. We hugged Tom, said goodbye and made our way to the door to walk across the tarmac. As I stepped outside and looked up into the sky, my stomach sank. The sky was black. The clouds were dancing all over the sky and the wind and rain were fierce!

"They cancelled the 8:00 flight while it was sunny and calm to send us up in THIS? Classic! Just classic!!!" I said as ran across the tarmac holding onto everything I could grab onto. By the time we reached the plane we were soaked and not a hair on our heads was where it was supposed to be. As we found our seats, they started the engines, quickly closed the door and told us to stay in our seats buckled up for the entire thirty-minute flight to Guatemala City. Duh! They didn't have to tell us that. We were bouncing all over the place and the plane was still on the ground!

We began taxiing down the runway and suddenly we jumped up into the air. It was as if we were on a trampoline and got a running start and bounced up into the sky. I could only imagine that it was the wind and airflow from the storm that jolted us up into the air like that. I felt someone grab my hand.

"Pray Jo! Pray! I am really scared!" Cheryl said through her silent tears. Fact was my insides were shaking too, but as I lowered my head to pray I heard those words again, *remember the rainbow!* My fear subsided once again and I reminded Dorothy and Jeff of the rainbow and what had been spoken to soothe my spirit.

Although the storm on the inside of us was calmed by those promising words, the storm raged on outside and the thirty minute roller-coaster ride to the City seemed like an eternity. Just a few minutes before we reached the City, the skies cleared and things grew calm and the landing was rather smooth. Hurricane Mitch had not debuted in Guatemala City yet, and for that we were extremely grateful.

Walking across the tarmac I questioned what would lie ahead. *What happens now, Lord? Where do we go from here?* I wondered to myself. The answers were about to unfold before my eyes. There was only one thing to do at this point-go to the Continental ticket counter and see what could be done with the ticket that I held in my hand that was absolutely worthless. It was the ticket to the flight I missed that would have had me halfway to Houston.

I told Jeff and Cheryl to stay with our luggage on the first level while I walked up to the second level to the ticket counter.

"Pray." I told them both.

"For what?" Jeff asked as I walked away. I stopped. Turned around slowly and looked him straight in the eyes.

"For a miracle!" I turned back around and headed up the steps.

I began to search for the Continental Airline ticket counter as soon as I reached the second level. It was total chaos! I never saw so many people standing in lines everywhere, well, except for the amusement parks on a nice summer day! Of course the line to Continental was as long as any line there. Why was I in any hurry? I had a ticket going NOWHERE!

As I walked over to the end of the line where at least a hundred people waited before me, I prayed to myself *Lord, please intervene! I don't know what to do!* As soon as I reached the end of the line and looked around all the people to see how far I still had to go, the lady behind the counter suddenly raised her head and looked right at me. She walked around from behind the counter and walked straight back to me. She never took her eyes off of me as she came. When she reached me she asked me in Spanish if she could help me.

"Habla usted Ingles?" I asked.

"Yes, I speak English," she answered.

I started to say something, but where would I begin? What exactly would I say? My eyes filled up with tears as I handed her the tickets. I couldn't utter a word at that moment because I knew if I did I would burst into uncontrollable weeping! She smiled sweetly at me and took the tickets. After glancing a moment at them, she suddenly looked up at me.

"I have a plane getting ready to depart right now to San Salvador. Where are the other two people traveling with you?"

"They are downstairs with our luggage, but we don't want to go to El Salvador!" I answered softly.

"Oh, I know, sweetie!" She giggled. "It is going to San Salvador to drop off some passengers and then it will reboard and fly straight to Houston! I can at least get you to Houston tonight. Do you want it?" she asked sweetly.

"Yes!" I answered before I had a chance to think about it. She picked up her two-way radio, said some things in Spanish to the person on the other end and motioned me to follow her.

"Take me to the other two passengers. We have to hurry!" she said as she turned to quickly walk to the stairs to the lower level.

When we reached Jeff and Cheryl she told them to grab the luggage and follow her. We practically ran through the airport to the gate. They were holding the plane for us, but couldn't hold it for long. Time was of the essence. Hurricane Mitch had picked up speed and gained strength.

"Do you have your airport tax handy?" she asked as we scurried to the gate.

"Yes!" the three of us answered in unison. We paid our airport tax to her in person on our way through the gate and onto the plane.

"Leave your check-in luggage here. We will tag it and put it in cargo hold. It will be waiting for you as you get off the plane in Houston. Oh, and have a safe trip home!" She smiled and waved as we walked down the corridor.

"Thank you so very much! God bless you!" I shouted back to her and then hurried onto the plane.

Several of the passengers applauded as we boarded and found our seats. We were placed in First Class. Those were the only seats left.

The door was shut immediately behind us. They were already a few minutes late departing because of us. We were pushed back away from the gate and then turned onto the tarmac to taxi to the runway. I could feel my heart beating fast and hard in my chest. I felt my whole body shaking. It had been a long day already and it was far from over!

We paused for a moment and then the captain came on and in Spanish and in English told us that we were cleared for takeoff and told the flight attendants to please be seated. We turned onto the runway, picked up speed and then lifted off the ground. Suddenly fear gripped me once again. *What am I doing? Why did I say I wanted this flight? I am heading AWAY from my country. I am going to El Salvador. El Salvador! Is El Salvador even SAFE? Oh, dear Jesus, what have I done?*

Almost immediately the question enters my head, *"What does El Salvador mean?"* With the answer came total peace. *The Savior! I'm flying into the Savior!* A smile replaced the concerned look on my face and I leaned my head back on the seat and rested for the rest of the flight. I was finally resting in my Savior!

I was jolted back to consciousness by the voice of the captain informing us we were starting our initial descent into San Salvador and the ding of the bell on the Fasten Seatbelts sign. I put my seat back up and glanced out the window to get a glimpse of this country I had never seen before. All I saw was black! There was nothing but black clouds out that window. It was a little bumpy, but not too bad. Then suddenly, as we burst through the clouds, I could see the ground. It was lusciously green. No sooner did we clear the clouds than I felt the bump of the tires upon the tarmac. We were on the ground. *Wow! Those clouds are low!* I thought to myself.

We were to get off the plane so they could clean up and prepare for the flight from here to Houston. We would be here about an hour and then head for the States. I decided to find a phone and give the missionaries back in the Petén a call. After all, they had no idea where we were. We were supposed to be in Guatemala City waiting for a flight back to the States. I also needed to contact Mom. The last I spoke with her we were stranded in the Petén and weren't sure what was going on.

I wasn't sure if I was going to reach the missionaries or not. I prayed that I could get through to them so that they would know we were all right and not be concerned for us. They had enough to think about with Hurricane Mitch getting ready to unleash his fury on them! It rang several times then finally I heard Dorothy's voice.

"Allo!" she said.

"Dorothy," I replied.

"JoeLynn!" she sounded shocked but relieved. "Where are you? Are you all right?"

"Yes, yes! We are fine. We are in San Salvador."

"San Salvador? What on earth are you doing in San Salvador?" She was extremely puzzled.

"It is a long story, but the short of it is that we are taking the long way home. We will be boarding our plane shortly and heading to Houston."

"Oh, well, praise God!" she hollered. "Then on home to Ohio?"

"Well, that remains to be seen. We aren't sure what happens once we get to Houston. We have to play it by ear, but we are headed in the right direction and will be out of harm's way!" I said without having a clue what was just ahead of us!

"Well, that is a relief!"

"What about you two? How is it going for you?" I asked.

"It is really starting to get bad here. I am amazed that the cell is working at all. It hasn't been working for the last couple of hours. By the way, I have some bad news."

"What?" I almost hated to ask.

"Remember the pastor we worked with in the village where we passed out all of the clothes and shoes?" She asked.

"Yes, the one with the new baby?"

"Yes. Well, we got word after you left that he was murdered yesterday."

"Murdered?" I was horrified.

"Yes. He was on his way to town on his bicycle to put the money he got from his crops in the bank when someone jumped him, stole his money and killed him with a macheté."

"Oh, how tragic!"

"Yes!" She said. "It is horrible! Please keep his wife, kids and congregation in prayer."

"I will. Well, I gotta go! I need to call Mom and tell her what's going on. Thanks for everything. We love you guys!"

"No, thank YOU! We appreciate all that you did while you were here. We love you too! God bless!"

I hung up and was about to start pushing the long list of numbers you have to push in order to make an international call from a calling card when I heard a familiar whistle. It was Jeff. He was several gates down and waving me to come on. *Darn! I can't call Mom to tell her what's going on.* I hurried down the hall to our gate.

They were already loading our plane.

"What? Why are we boarding so early? We aren't supposed to leave for another forty-five minutes." I asked.

"Take a look outside!" Jeff pointed out the window.

"Oh, my God!"

"We are boarding now to try and get out of here before it gets any worse. They are closing the airport as soon as we take off."

"Dear, Lord, have mercy!" I said in disbelief.

It was black all around. Clouds swirling around, palms trees bending over touching the ground and things flying everywhere. We got loaded onto the plane. I was once again over the wing while Jeff and Cheryl were placed in the back of the plane. The very last row as a matter of fact. They didn't even have a window, which turned out to be a blessing for Cheryl! I looked out my window and swallowed hard. The plane was shaking and it was no wonder why. The wings were flapping in the high winds like the wings of a bird.

The captain came on and gave this long message in Spanish and then gave the same one in English. Toward the end of his message several people mumbled something under their breath while others just said "Ohhhh!" He informed us we were in for a rough flight. He instructed the flight attendants to stay buckled up in their seats until he gave the signal they could move around. He told each of us to stay in our seats and get up for no reason unless he turned the Fasten Seatbelts sign off. Then he said we would be flying for about an hour through Hurricane Mitch. *Oh, my Lord! Is that safe?* Of course we were rerouted around it as much as possible, but we would be flying the first hour through the outer bands of Mitch.

We were given the permission to take off and so we started down the runway, picking up speed. Then we lifted off and for the next hour we were thrown and bounced around the sky. People were screaming. Children and even some adults were crying. The young woman behind me was extremely scared and kept cursing every time the plane would shake and drop several hundred feet at a time. If that was not enough, several passengers were vomiting too!

I prayed hard and continuously! I kept asking the Lord to forgive the cursing of the young woman behind me and to please have mercy on us all and protect us from this devastating storm. Watching the display of violent, angry clouds throwing bolts of lightning across the sky was terrifying enough, but add to the visual the feeling of being bounced around the sky like a steely in a pinball machine and you have one hellacious situation. I admit that it was one of the most terrifying experiences of my life. There were moments when I really believed the plane would literally shake apart, lose an engine or just be plummeted to the earth. When the fear came flooding in and I was on the brink of bursting into tears that still small voice reminded me yet once more: *remember the rainbow!*

Knowing that He had protected us from the storm flying to the Petén, protected us from the witch doctor's spell, protected us from the malaria that was all around us, protected us from the Galgos bus, and protected us from the storm flying to Guatemala City, I knew that He was protecting us from the hurricane. Mitch was no match for the awesome God that chose to covenant with us! I leaned my head back and began to understand why God sent the rainbow. It was an awesome thing to see, but it was so much more than that. It was a visual of how we were always in the center of His covenant of protection. Nothing could by any means break through His barrier of protection and harm us. I will NEVER forget that image of our plane in the center of that rainbow. Maybe this is how Noah felt when he stepped off the ark and beheld the first rainbow of God's covenant.

Almost an hour exactly after we took off, the plane went from violently turbulent skies to the sudden peacefully calm. Immediately the captain came on and informed us we were out of the grips of Mitch and that it would be smooth flying from that point on to Houston. I looked out the window and could see the lights of ships on the waters of the Gulf below. Ahead of us the moon was shining bright in the clear skies over the gulf just off the coast of Mexico. Behind us was the twisting, churning devastation of Hurricane Mitch.

The flight attendants got up and began to serve us drinks and a snack. We were going to be all right. Children quit crying. Adults quit vomiting. Desperate prayers for deliverance turned to thankful praise for protection. Oh, and the young lady behind me; she remembered vocabulary words other than four letter curse words. The muscles began to relax in my body. My heartbeat and respirations slowed to a normal rhythm and pace. My tightly clenched fists finally relaxed and opened.

As I was whispering words of thanks for divine protection and prayers for what was ahead of us, I had no idea of the total devastation that was behind us! Four days after its birth as a tropical depression, Hurricane Mitch quickly grew to a category five hurricane on the Saffir-Simpson Hurricane Scale. It first made landfall on October 29, 1998 in Trujillo, Honduras after wreaking havoc in the Antilles. Two days later it turned its fury loose on Guatemala and Belize before hitting the Yucatan Peninsula. Mitch then weakened to a tropical depression before heading out to the warm waters of the Gulf. In the Gulf Mitch gained strength again and hit Key West as Tropical Storm Mitch.

Hurricane Mitch killed more people than any other hurricane in over 200 years. More than three million people were left homeless or their lives viciously altered and over five billion dollars in damage done. As I looked out the window of the Boeing 727, and beheld the monstrous killer behind me, I had no clue of the devastation just behind its veil. I once again whispered a prayer of thanks for the protection God had provided, but it would be quite some time before I would realize just what a miracle it truly was.

According to the National Climatic Data Center Hurricane Mitch, at 990 mb of pressure and sustained winds of 180 mph, quickly became the deadliest storm to hit the western hemisphere since the "Great Hurricane" of 1780. It would take over a week before the magnitude of that storm and all of its destruction would rock the rest of the world. Statistics reported over 11,000 dead and untold thousands missing. Due to the lack of vital records in these developing countries, the actual total would NEVER be known.

Total rainfall was reported as high as 75 inches for the entire storm. Floods resulting from the enormous rainfall and the accompanying mud slides virtually destroyed the entire infrastructure of Honduras, and devastated widespread areas of Nicaragua, Guatemala, Belize, and El Salvador. Entire villages and their inhabitants were swept away in seconds by the torrents of flood waters and unfathomable mud that came rushing down the mountainsides. Hundreds of thousands of homes were destroyed.

I laid my head back on my seat and closed my tired eyes. My fatigued mind played through each of the events of the day like a movie in a VCR. Occasionally, it would pause to contemplate on the details of certain events. Although my body was exhausted, my mind was too stimulated and my thoughts too emotionally charged to allow me to sleep. Before I realized it, my thoughts were interrupted by the voice of our pilot. He was pleased to announce our initial descent into the Houston area. We weren't in Ohio yet, but thank God, we were in the States! For all intents and purposes, we were home! *What happens from here, God, only You know*, I thought to myself. He had brought us this far safely and I knew He would get us the rest of the way home safely too. Of that I was completely convinced!

Inside the terminal was total chaos! Thousands of weary travelers were stranded. Flights had arrived from all over Central America. Passengers were fleeing to America to escape the deadly grip of Hurricane Mitch. It created pandemonium inside the Houston airport. Flights delayed. Flights cancelled. Flights overbooked and passengers bumped. Every hotel, motel, bed and breakfast was full. Every rental car was taken. Even still, thousands were stranded at the Houston airport trying to get home or to family or friends where they could stay until it was safe to go back to their homes. If they had homes to go back to at all!

We were three more weary travelers added to the thousands already there. I told Jeff and Cheryl to find a seat and stay with the luggage and I would stand in line. It was a good forty-five minutes before I finally reached the lady behind the counter. She had been there since 4:00 that morning and was exhausted also, but this crisis meant nobody went home.

She didn't smile when she hollered, "Next!" She didn't even look up. "Can I help you?" she asked robotically.

"I sure hope so, Ma'am." I said with the last bit of hope I had left in me.

She looked up at me. I smiled a tired smile. I knew she was tired too. "I really doubt I can, but I'll take a look."

"I guess that is all I can hope for then." I said with a smile.

"I'm sorry, but there are no flights available until Tuesday to Columbus." She looked me straight in the eyes. She was used to being yelled at and even cursed at all day long.

I took a long slow breath. "I don't know what to do." I could feel the tears welling up in my eyes, but I fought hard to keep them back. I swallowed. "I know you have been here all day and you are exhausted too. I have stood here in line and heard the verbal abuse you have taken and I know it is not your fault. But ma'am, we have been in the Petén of Guatemala for ten days on a medical mission's trip. We have come face to face with a witch doctor, have been hit by a bus and almost plane wrecked three times. We have been traveling for the last twelve hours; we are out of money and have no place to go. All we want is to get home to our families. Is there absolutely nothing you can do?" I knew my bottom lip was quivering as she looked at me with a now softened expression.

"Honey, I wish I could, I really do, but it will take a miracle to get you home before Tuesday."

"Well, that's ok. I believe in miracles. It took several miracles to get us this far." I began to pray under my breath. *Father, you have brought us this far, and I know You didn't get us here just to leave us stranded. Take us on home, Lord.*

She looked back down at her computer and began punching away at the keys. She looked back and forth from the monitor to our tickets. Then she let out a big slow sigh. "I'm so sorry, Miss Daugherty, there is absolutely nothing I can do. I have even checked other airlines for you."

I looked down for a moment. I was praying. *Lord, I know this isn't it. There must be something…* Before I could finish my thought in prayer it came to me. "What about Cincinnati?"

"Excuse me?" she said puzzled.

"What about the Cincinnati airport? Is there anything available through Cincinnati?" I asked. "It is the same distance from our house to Cincinnati as it is to Columbus."

"Let me check." With that she went back to clicking away at her keyboard. "Yes, oh my goodness, yes there is!" she said excitedly.

164

"But it doesn't leave until 8:00 in the morning." We both looked up at the clock at the same time. 11:07 pm. We had nine hours to wait in the airport.

"That would be wonderful, Ma'am!" I said and forced a smile through an involuntary sigh. "We will just camp out here until then."

Her eyes searched my face. For what I don't know. I have no idea what was going through her head. She looked back down at her computer and began to type away again. Then she looked up and said, "Excuse me just a moment." Then she disappeared into a small office behind the neighboring kiosk.

I could tell that people behind me were getting impatient. A few choice words were being thrown around. However, before I was hung by an angry mob she appeared again with a great big satisfied grin. "I'm afraid I cannot let you camp out here for the night."

My heart sunk! *What?* I could not understand why not and I was really confused by the smile. My face must have shown my dismay.

"That is why I am giving you the last two rooms at the airport Sheraton and two meal vouchers a piece. One for dinner tonight and one for breakfast in the morning. Go get your travel buddies, get you something to eat and a good night's rest." she said as she handed me the tickets and vouchers. "I already have you checked in. You can take the tram to the entrance of the hotel."

"You did it! You found that miracle!" I said as my eyes filled up with tears. "Thank you so much. God bless you real big!"

She smiled. "I didn't find that miracle. It found me!"

I wanted to give her a great big hug, but I knew we were both about to be hung by the ever restless crowd. I thanked her again and turned to walk away. *Wow, thank You, Father!*

Our rooms were next door to each other. I stuck my key card in the door and opened it. I stepped in and suddenly stopped. *Oh, my Lord!* It was a king suite. Jeff and Cheryl had one too. *This is exceeding abundantly above all I could ask for or even think of,* I thought to myself as I walked in and laid my luggage on the bed. "Thank You, Father! You did so much more than I could ever have expected," I said out loud as I collapsed onto the bed beside my luggage.

I called Mom immediately and let her know where we were. She was more than ready to hear from us. It had been sixteen hours since she heard from me in the Petén. The last she knew we were there trying to get to Guatemala City and had no idea what would happen to us when we got there. I explained how we had no time to contact her from the City since we were hustled to the plane being held for us at the gate. She was just thankful we were in the States.

"This is even better for you, Sis," Mom said. "Now you can relax in a hot tub, get a good night's rest and fly home a bit more relaxed."

We said good night and shared "I love you" with each other and I commenced to running that hot bath. It sounded so good. I went in and ordered a light meal for room service to bring up since it had been about eighteen hours since we ate. The bath felt better than any I had ever taken before. I almost fell asleep in it. Just as I was putting on my robe that was provided for me by the hotel, there was a knock on the door and I heard the infamous words, "Room Service."

166

Our flight from Houston to Cincinnati was so smooth. It was a beautiful, sunny day in late fall. November the second to be exact. It would be a day that I would NEVER forget. The flight seemed longer than usual, but only because I was so much more than ready to get home. It seemed like I had left home a year ago rather than just ten days ago.

We landed safely in Cincinnati and I called Mom from my cell phone to let her know we landed and would be heading straight home. I was looking so forward to telling her, "I'll see you in two hours."

The two hour drive from Cincinnati to Portsmouth seemed to last even longer! Good Lord, I just want to be home and see my family! But thank You for bringing us home safe. *Thank You for all You have done. I cannot even begin to express my gratitude.*

A few days later I received the tragic news of the crash of the twin engine DC-3 belonging to Living Waters Teaching in Quetzaltenango. It went down in the mountains of Guatemala during Hurricane Mitch. On it were eighteen members of a medical mission's team. Eleven of the eighteen were killed. Miraculously, seven walked away. Of those killed were a few of our friends from Bible school and fellow missionaries to Guatemala, Jim Zirkle, his son, Jimmy, his son-in-law, Chris Hamberger and Living Water staff member, Raul Jacobs. The seven others killed were members of a medical mission's team from the States.

It was a sobering and humbling thought to recall how miraculously God brought Jeff and Cheryl and I home safely despite the witch doctor, the malaria carrying mosquitoes, the bus accident and the hurricane. What factors determined our miraculous deliverance and the Zirkles' tragedy? Why did eleven die and seven walk away from the same accident? It wasn't for me to determine. Some of those questions would never be answered. Some would be answered a short time later. Nevertheless, I came to realize during those ten days in the Petén that my God would never leave me or forsake me. I learned there was NOTHING that could harm me when God said He would keep me safe and well.

Chapter
Six

It had been only seven months since I returned from the Petén in Guatemala. I had not been on any other trips. There were none on the schedule either. I ran my own daycare in my home where I took care of six children. I had been running my own daycare for four years. I loved watching the children and I had become very attached to them and their parents. Even though it was good money, there was something lacking in my life. There was a longing in my heart for something more. Much more. But what?

One day, while I was visiting with my mother at the Church office, I picked up a DVD that was lying on her desk. It was from the Bible school my parents and I had attended in Broken Arrow, Oklahoma. The front of it said, "An Important Announcement from Lynette Hagin."

"Mom, what is this?" I asked as I picked it up.

"Sis, you'll just have to watch it yourself."

"All right then. I will." I put it in my purse, told Mom good-bye and left the office to head home.

It was a very hot and humid day in June of 1999. The ladies I normally walked with in the evenings were either away on vacation or occupied with family activities. It was too hot outside to go walking this evening. So, I opted to sit down and watch the DVD. I put the disk in, sat down on the couch, kicked my feet up on the ottoman and began to watch. It didn't take but a few minutes to realize I was meant to watch it. The first few words captured my attention immediately. My feet came off the ottoman, hit the floor and I found myself on the edge of my seat. Something was beginning to stir inside of me.

Mrs. Lynette Hagin had the microphone. She was making the announcement that Rhema would be offering a new third year class; the Rhema School of World Missions. As soon as she said those words, something shot through every fiber of my being like lightning. I began to shake and cry at the same time. There was no doubt that I was meant to attend this School of World Missions. *But how? The question was just a fleeting thought. I guess if God wants me to go then He will have to make a way!*

The next day I went to visit Mom. She was at the church. I went into her office and sat down across the desk from her in my favorite chair. I just looked at her for a moment.

"What?" she asked.

I laid the DVD on her desk. I looked at her for a moment more.

"Y-y-e-e-s-s?" she said slowly, dropping her head, raising her eyebrows and looking back at me waiting for a response.

I was searching for the right words to say. I wasn't even sure what was going to come out when I finally did open my mouth. Suddenly I blurted out, "That's for me! I'm supposed to go!"

"Yea, I know. I watched it when it first arrived. I knew you were supposed to go." She finally grinned at me. "Now what?" she asked.

"I don't know."

"Well, I think you better be figuring it out. It's June and classes start in September. You can live with your brother. The Church will pay your monthly tuition, but you are going to have to get a job as soon as possible."

"I have a job!" I said laughing.

"Uh, I mean in TULSA!" she said laughing too.

I'll never forget the way I felt the day I pulled into Tulsa. It was August 9, 1999. I was excited, but nervous. I hadn't been to school in eighteen years. I also wondered what my future held. *Where will I go from here, Lord?* I thought to myself as I drove through Broken Arrow, Oklahoma on the way to my brother's house.

My brother left me instructions on how to get into his house through the garage. He would not be home for another couple of hours. I took all of my belongings to the spare bedroom and laid them down. I was too tired from traveling to put things away immediately.

I went into the living room to relax and watch some television. I dropped the remote on the floor and as I bent over to pick it up someone whistled. I turned suddenly expecting to see my brother who may have come home early, but found no one there. Just Buddy, my brother's Pekingese. Buddy sat there looking up at me. I thought I must be hearing things. So I bent over to pick it up again and again I heard the same wolf call.

I turned around immediately and said, "Doug, are you messing with me?" That was not uncommon for my brother to do. Suddenly I heard someone whistle for the dog and Buddy went running into the dining room. I followed him. He sat on the floor looking up at a sheet that seemed to be covering something. I lifted the sheet to find a white cockatoo looking back at me, who suddenly began laughing in a man's voice. "Hello," he said.

"Well, hello." I answered back.

I had no idea my brother had a bird, an obnoxiously friendly flirt of a bird. He started talking and wouldn't shut up. All I wanted was to relax in front of the television and enjoy the peace and quiet before my brother and sister-in-law got home. The bird decided he rather enjoyed having company and tried to strike up a conversation with me.

Around two hours later my brother came home and was greeted with a warm "Hello. How you doing?" My brother returned the greeting. "Hello, Polo! How YOU doing?" "Hi, Sis!" he said, coming over to give me a hug.

"Good. But, uh, I didn't know you had a bird."

"Oh, Polo? He belongs to one of the girls, but he might as well be Lema's."

"Oh, yeah? Well, he is a big flirt! You should have warned me about him."

"Oh, he must've whistled at ya," he said laughing.

"Yes, and it about scared the bejeebers out of me!"

I did get a job in Tulsa and it was perfect! I got a job working in a doctor's office as a medical assistant. During the summer I worked every day, all day. Once my classes started in the fall I worked afternoons. I gained experience and knowledge that would help me later in life.

As a result of working for this doctor I was blessed in another way. Things were rather crowded at my brother's house and often busy and loud with kids and grandkids coming and going. It was also a long distance from where I worked. One day the doctor called me into his office with a proposition. His mother-in-law lived alone and had a stroke. She had to go to a nursing home. She owned a home and they did not want it to sit empty. She had all of her belongings in the house. So, the doctor asked me if I would be willing to "house sit." I could live in the house rent free with all utilities paid and use her furniture. It was a beautiful three-bedroom home located halfway between missions' school and work. What a tremendous blessing!

I'm not sure what I was expecting, but the year at missions' school was like nothing I could have imagined. In fact, it was nothing like the two years I spent at Bible school eighteen years earlier. The only thing I did know was that I was supposed to go. I knew that God would meet me there.

Our instructor, Joe Duininck, taught us the first semester. He taught on subjects like Cross Cultural Issues in Missions and Preparation for the Mission Field.

As part of Preparation for the Mission Field, we had a three-day survival trip. I was not in the least prepared for the experiences of those three days! As soon as we arrived in the wilderness of Oklahoma we learned how to work together as a team. We were given tasks that we could not complete unless we worked together. It wasn't until we learned teamwork, that we were taught how to survive alone in the wild. We were instructed on how to build our own shelters, latrines, and fires with no matches. One night our survival instructor took us to a remote area and told us to get out of the vehicle. He gave us instructions, coordinates and a compass before he left. We had to work together in order to find our way back to camp.

In those three days of survival training we had to climb a mountain, repel our way down and then conquer fear by doing the "Zip Line." We slept in shelters we built out of a sheet of plastic, tree branches and other items from the woods around us. We endured an intense storm and torrential downpours. On top of all that, we learned to cook and eat what we could find. All lessons I would be drawing from for years to come!

During our year at the Rhema School of World Missions Joe Duininck had invited missionaries from all over the world as guest speakers. They shared their testimonies and real life experiences as well as the lessons they learned from those experiences.

I gleaned so much from each and every one of them. However, my favorite guest missionary, by far, was the Reverend Joseph

Purcell. He, his wife and four children, were at the time, missionaries to the Russian Far East. Little did I know then that I would spend a month with him and his family in Khabarovsk, Russia. I never imagined myself in Russia, but when the time came I was more than ready to go.

As part of the requirements to graduate from the Rhema School of World Missions, we had to go on a thirty-day internship to a foreign country and work with missionaries who were known to the school. I had planned to go to the Darien Jungle in Panama, but I decided to go to Guatemala instead.

Soon after my arrival there I became unhappy. I really didn't know why at the time. When I spoke with Mom on the phone one night after I had been there for a few days, she asked me how I liked it. I told her how I felt. She asked what it was I didn't like about it. I could not answer her right away. I did not know myself.

It was not all work while I was there. I had always loved to ride the rides at the fair at home so I was game for the rides here during Carnival. Little did I realize that they did not hold these carnies to the same standards as in the States. I found that out the hard way.

Tracy stood close by watching me as I gave the ticket to the man and found my seat on the ride. The ride was called the Tagada. I saw it running with no one in it. They were testing it out before they loaded it. It looked fun. So I was one of the first in line. We were all seated in this round saucer like ride with no seat belts or harnesses. I figured gravity would hold us in place.

The ride started out slow. Then got a little faster. Then even faster. No problem. This was great. Then suddenly it started to jump up and down. Side to side. Immediately people began to be thrown into the center of the floor. We tried holding on to whatever we could find. We tried bracing ourselves. It was useless. We soon became human popcorn! Many were screaming and everyone was sliding into each other. We were being thrown into the air and back down again. Many times on top of others. I started grasping for whatever I could get ahold of to stabilize myself. Arms and legs were flying in attempts to grab anything to hold onto. Dignity went flying as we did.

After what seemed like an eternity the ride quit popping up and down and just started spinning around. We were all slung to the sides of the ride, except this time we were under the seats instead of in them. As the ride came to a stop I realized I had something clenched in my hand. It was a tennis shoe. Not my tennis shoe, however, it belonged to someone else. I apparently grabbed it and ripped it off of someone's foot in an attempt to hold on. I held it up as I exited the ride. The young man came running over and took it from me with a perplexed look on his face. He probably wondered why I ripped it off his foot in the first place.

When I reached Tracy, who was standing in the grass close to the exit, she was bent over in laughter. She couldn't talk for laughing so hard. She said it was one of the funniest things she had ever watched. Needless to say, I never rode that ride again and sported around bruises for a week. Tracy and I still laugh about that when we think about it. She and her family are still missionaries in Xela and we still keep in touch.

When I returned to Tulsa after that internship I was asked if I had made a decision about the offer to take a permanent position with a large ministry in Guatemala. I graciously declined. She asked why I decided not to take it. Suddenly, I knew why. I heard these words come out of my mouth that I had never said before. "Because I am called to primitive missions."

"What do you mean?" She looked puzzled.

Actually, I really didn't know. It was the first time I heard those words. It was the first time I had thought about it. Then as I spoke the revelation came.

"I mean…well, I desire to go to those who have never yet heard the Gospel. I want to go where no one has gone before, to those who are tucked away in a jungle somewhere. I feel called to those who have nothing, have no one and who have never been reached."

I was as shocked as she was to hear those words. I didn't know before why I wasn't happy in Xela. However, now the light was turned on and I suddenly knew. Although I never thought about it before, it was very true. Every word I had just spoken came straight from the inner most regions of my heart. I had no idea how those words would one day come to pass.

The year in missions' school was a year of divine appointments. I met people that would be instrumental in shaping my future. People that would become a part of my life long support system. People I would never forget. Those individuals made deposits in me that I draw from to this day. I was inspired and fortified by their courage and strength. I cannot even begin to put into words everything I experienced, learned and came away with from my year at the Rhema School of World Missions. Much of who I am today and the kind of missionary I am is because of that year.

As I said earlier, I spent a month in the Russian Far East with Joe Purcell and his family. I had the privilege of working with their children's ministry and teaching at an interdenominational Children's Ministry Conference. I taught Children's Ministry in their Bible school and visited a couple of orphanages. That was an experience that had such an impact on me that it would influence the direction my life was about to take.

The last week of my stay in Khabarovsk I had the privilege of participating in a Minister's Conference hosted by Joe Purcell Ministries. Ministers from Russia, China, Korea and the United States gathered together in that cold, damp auditorium the first week of April in 2001. The guest speakers for the Conference were the Directors of Rhema Italy, Tony and Patsy Cameneti, as well as James and Cathy Creek. It was a wonderful time of powerful praise and worship, and of power-packed preaching followed by miracles, signs and wonders.

On the last day of the conference I woke up feeling the need to be alone. I knew something was going on inside me but wasn't quite sure what it is was. I told the lady with me to go on to the morning meetings without me. I told her I would I would catch up with her that evening in time for the last service. I spent the day alone in my hotel room praying and crying out to God for direction. I could feel change was coming, but had no idea what the future held for me.

Time passed by quickly and it was soon time to leave for the evening service. So, I grabbed my coat, headed out the door and down the street to the corner where I would board a tram. That particular tram would drop me off in front of the convention center. It was about fifteen minutes away.

As I stood there on the corner waiting for the tram I had no idea what I was about to experience ten minutes up the tramline. I climbed aboard as soon as the door opened and squeezed my way in amongst the crowd of people already aboard. Only in the United States is there an unofficial eighteen inch personal space rule. So, the door closed on the multitude of us inside the tram and away it rattled down the line.

It was April in Khabarovsk and that meant it was cold. Freezing cold. There was snow on the ground and the grey skies threatened more snow was coming. The tram wound its way through the city streets and stopped from time to time to let passengers on and off.

There were now four more stops before the convention center. The tramline crossed over the highway below just up ahead. It was approximately 300 to 400 feet to the highway and the cars speeding along below us. Just as the tram started onto the overpass something jerked the tram and suddenly we started to lean to the left. People were screaming and falling into each other as the tram began to tip over onto the highway below. All I could do was holler the Name of Jesus. Just as I did the tram stood upright and continued on its way.

Everyone suddenly became quiet and looked at each other. I am sure they were wondering what just happened. I was in the back by this time and I turned to look out the window. There in the middle of the overpass was a section of track about eight feet long that was missing. Gone. I have no idea what happened to the track, but I am sure that as I called the Name of Jesus an angel was dispatched to grab hold of that tram and sit it upright on the track.

The next thing I know we were stopped in front of the convention center and I got out. I walked into the auditorium and found my seat on the second row. I turned to my friend from missions' school, which accompanied me to Russia, I was shaking like a leaf.

"What's wrong?" she inquired. "You look like you've seen a ghost."

"Not a ghost," I answered. "But I am pretty sure I encountered an angel."

"What?" she asked, looking like she just saw one.

I began to quickly share with her what just happened. Just as I finished, the guest ministers came in and sat down in the front row.

Just before the service started, Patsy Cameneti turned around and gave me a scripture she said the Lord had given her to share with me. She then spoke a powerful word to me confirming what I had on my heart that no one else knew. That scripture and word of encouragement set my feet on a new course that would change my life completely. It directed me toward my divine destiny.

It would be an eleven-hour flight across the Pacific and the International Date Line before I landed at LAX. Then fly to Atlanta and on to Columbus. During that flight across the Pacific, I asked God to show me His plan for my life. In the early morning hours, while everyone else was asleep, God spoke to my heart and instructed me to go to nursing school. How? I had wanted to go to nursing school for years. Pretty much my whole life! I was never able to go. My family made too much money to get grants and not enough to afford the tuition. No further instructions came. He simply said, "Go."

Six weeks after returning from Russia I was sitting in Chemistry 121. My mind was full of questions, but I was so excited to be on my way to fulfilling a lifelong dream, to go to college and become a nurse. It was something I always wanted to do, but never had the chance. My life had taken many twists and turns that I never imagined, or that I ever saw coming. Suddenly there I was. I looked around me. *What am I doing here?* I thought. *I am thirty-eight years old. These kids are right out of high school. How am I going to make it? Who am I kidding?*

I was also majoring in English with an emphasis on writing. God placed special people in my life during those years in college. Professors who shaped my career as a nurse and professors who encouraged me to pursue writing as well. I would never have made it through those four years of college had it not been for the awesome people God placed in my life. Again, I am what I am today because of the preparation I received during those years. Preparation that only God knew I needed.

I have come to realize that it was a matter of timing. Each of those preparations was prioritized in a way only God could. He saw the beginning from the end. He had my life planned before I was born. I also realized that the desires in my heart that I thought conflicted with each other, actually complimented one another. I just had to let God bring them all together as only He could.

So much happened to me during those years in nursing school. I gained confidence in ways I never imagined possible. I gained knowledge that would become the foundation of everything that I would do and I gained a love and respect for research. Research that I will need to complete the final phase of the life God has called me to live. The plan, the dream I was born to fulfill. The work I was born to do.

Chapter
Seven

I learned of Mercy Mission Teams from a friend that I met during my year at the Rhema School of World Missions. I joined them for the first time in 2002. That was the first time I had the privilege of meeting John and Lottie Hall, missionaries to El Salvador. Relationships and bonds were made on that trip that would continue on for years and lead many of us to the Amazon Jungle of Peru.

In May of 2007, I received an email from Lottie. She asked me if I would be traveling with Mercy Mission Teams to the Amazon. My heart began to beat faster as I read the word Amazon. My father and I always talked about going to the Amazon. We dreamed of being on the Amazon River and visiting the villages along its banks. There wasn't any information. Just the question, "Are you going to the Amazon?"

Although I had no more information, my answer was emphatically, "YES!" I replied to her email immediately. I needed more information. I knew I was going. Somehow I knew God would make a way. It was one thing my father and I talked about for years. The call and desire to take the Word of God to the Amazon Jungle.

Lottie returned an email to me within a couple of days with the information that she had. I would have to contact the director of Mercy Mission Teams, Dr. Robert Harman. I traveled with him and the team to El Salvador, where I met Lottie. Now the team was going to the Amazon Jungle of Peru. The trip was scheduled for the last two weeks of July.

There was so much to be done in such a short time. I needed to raise money for the trip, and obtain much needed items for our stay in the jungle. This was going to be ten days and nine nights in the jungle. Eating, sleeping, bathing and everything else in the jungle. I needed to be prepared. That meant purchasing a jungle hammock.

I needed mosquito repellant and lots of it. I was also required to get the Yellow Fever vaccine and I needed to make sure my Tetanus shot was up to date. I checked my passport to make sure it was current and checked online to see if a visa was needed for travel in Peru.

It took the entire seven months to get ready for the trip. I had a list of things to purchase to be prepared for what we might encounter in the jungle. With all the preparations that needed to be made, the time passed by quickly. It was now a couple of days before departure. I was packed and ready to go. My mom had a prayer cloth ready for me to take. I would never leave home without one. There were many times I would take that anointed cloth out and use it for myself or someone else. After all, if it was good enough for Paul the Apostle then it was definitely good enough for me! Paul was my Biblical hero.

Talk about a real missionary, he was my example. I just prayed I did not have to be shipwrecked or beaten like he was.

I took my luggage to service Sunday to be prayed over. I learned quickly during all my other travels to have my luggage prayed over. Too many times before I had lost or damaged luggage. Since I started having my luggage prayed for by my Church, I never had another lost or damaged piece. Nothing was ever stolen or confiscated by immigrations or customs either. So, I brought in my carry-on and check in luggage and laid it all up front until the end of the service when my pastors and Church family would pray over it.

Several of the ladies in my church volunteered to pray an hour each day for me. I was going to be covered in prayer during this trip. None of us had any idea what to expect. We were aware of impending dangers, but this is what we all had been believing for. This was the desire of my heart and the desire my father had in his heart for years. Now, I was going to actually fulfill that desire. Only God knew where this trip would lead.

Chapter
Eight

I had butterflies in my stomach as I sat at the gate in the Houston Airport. The flight from Houston to Lima was six hours long. I would be the second one to arrive in Lima. Lottie would be there first. She was flying in from San Salvador and would arrive a couple of hours before me. We were told that we would be staying at the Lima Sheraton Hotel and that there would be a shuttle from the hotel at the airport to pick us up and take us to the hotel. No problem! That sounded easy enough.

I had been flying internationally now for sixteen years and was used to customs and immigrations. The flight to Lima was long, but not the longest flight I had experienced. I was too excited to sleep. I did close my eyes for a little while and imagined what this trip was going to be like. Realistically, I had no idea what I was up against!

Finally, the plane landed at Jorge Chavez International Airport in Lima, Peru. Once again, it was the usual Passport, Immigrations and Customs routine. Nothing scary or out of the ordinary. I picked up my luggage and proceeded to the airport exit. First, I had to push a button. If the light was green, I could pass through without search. If it was red, I would have to stop and have my luggage searched and be asked a dozen questions. Green! I was relieved and passed on through.

Once inside the main lobby of the airport they were holding up signs with the names of hotels and passengers. No sign of the Sheraton Lima shuttle driver. After searching the crowd for a few minutes with no sign of my hotel. I found my way to the Airport Information Desk. I asked about a shuttle to the Sheraton Lima Hotel. She didn't know of any. She called the hotel. No shuttle service. *Huh? How can that be? Dr. Bob said there would be a shuttle.*

There was nothing left to do but hail a taxi. I had to get to the hotel. I headed toward the door to find a taxi driver. I was once again waylaid by a multitde of drivers vying for my business. Finally, a man walked up and asked me where I needed to go. I told him the Sheraton Lima Hotel. He got on his walkie talkie and then told me it would be twenty-five soles. At the time, with the exchange rate being 3.96 to 1, the taxi was about six and half dollars. That was not bad, so I took it!

The taxi driver pulled up and loaded my luggage and away we drove into the night. Suddenly, I began to wonder if I had made a mistake. I guess I should have prayed about getting a safe taxi driver. We drove for more than thirty minutes. In some really rough neighborhoods. I was certain he was taking me for a ride and I don't mean a taxi ride to the Sheraton! I began to pray really hard. *Oh, Lord, please help me. Please get me to the Sheraton Lima safe!*

Suddenly, in the distant darkness I saw a light. The light of the Sheraton Lima. *Praise God!* I drew in a great sigh of relief. We pulled up and he opened my door like a gentleman and then unloaded my luggage. By this time the doorman at the hotel came up with a luggage cart and took it from there. I paid the driver for the ride and then gave him a tip for handling the luggage. I followed the doorman inside to the desk.

I was greeted by the beautiful smile of a lovely Latin lady. I told her who I was with and she called the room Lottie was in and told her I was waiting in the lobby. In just a couple of minutes I was greeted by a familiar face. "Lottie!" I hollered as I ran to hug her. "JoJo!" She greeted back. I was called JoJo by the team members.

A couple of hours later we saw a taxi pull up and another familiar face stepped out. Bro. Butch! His real name is Joseph Sellers. Following closely behind him was a woman I had never met. Every hair was in place and she walked rather tall and stately. *Hmmm. I'm not sure Miss Priss is going to make it in the jungle.* I thought to myself. Little did I know that "Miss Priss" and I would become close friends and end up working together in our own medical missions organization.

Brother Butch introduced his traveling companion and fellow church member as Miss Charlene Barnes. She lived in Maryland, too. It was so good seeing Lottie and Bro. Butch again and meeting the newest member of our team. A team that would become family by the end of the trip!

Finally, at 1:00 in the morning, an airport shuttle arrived and the rest of the team unloaded. Diane Hooker, Jim Harman, who was Dr. Bob's brother, Randy Miller, Jim Thomlinson and Dr. Bob completed the team. We had all arrived safely.

We talked for a few minutes and then headed on to our rooms. We were all exhausted and had a busy day tomorrow. We were gathering for a breakfast meeting in the morning at 7:30 and then check out and head to the airport for our flight to the jungle. We all were so excited, but equally tired at that point. We exchanged hugs, good nights and headed to our rooms.

We all met downstairs, went to the breakfast Dr. Bob opened with prayer and we ate as he started discussing the plans. He gave us an agenda for that day. He was not sure what the rest of the time there held. Not one of us had been to the Amazon before or had worked with this particular missionary and his wife who were directors of Youth With a Mission or YWAM for short.

During that breakfast meeting Dr. Bob looked at me and said, "You know, JoJo, you could do what I do."

"What do you mean?" I asked.

"I mean you could run your own medical missions organization."

When he said that my heart rate increased and my stomach got butterflies once again. I had begun thinking about starting my own medical missions organization, but I sure didn't know if that was God or me. I definitely didn't believe I could really do it. It was just a thought I had been entertaining in my head and in my dreams. Now, I knew, this was confirmation. It really was God leading me. *But how?*

It was time to board the plane to Iquitos. We had no idea what we were about to see on our two hour flight to the Heart of the Amazon. As soon as we lifted off of the runway, we turned around over the Pacific Ocean. Only then could we see in the daylight hours that Lima was an oceanside city built on the top of a mountain.

No sooner had we leveled off, and reached cruising altitude than we could see the tops of the Andes Mountains peeking through the morning clouds. They reminded me of scoops of chocolate ice cream covered in marshmallow cream. It was a spectacular view. The further away from Lima we got, the more the clouds cleared so that we could see all the way down to the mountain paths. Villages were sprinkled up and down the mountainside. Occasionally, I would notice a mountain river winding its way down the mountains.

We flew smoothly over the Andes. After about an hour the mountains faded into the distance and gave way to a thick carpet of green. The Amazon Jungle! What a difference from the scene I had enjoyed for the past hour. Then in the distance I saw it. The snake winding its way through the lush green carpet. The Amazon River! It was very brown. Such a contrast to the dark green jungle. I was spellbound, yet I was still able to snap pictures from my new Canon camera. I was taking home pictures for my family and friends to see. After all, I had no idea when I might ever experience this again.

I could feel the plane slow its air speed and begin the intial descent. The more we descended the larger the trees below us became. I could see little wooden huts through the dense trees. More frequently I began to see the smoke of a village fire rising through the trees to greet us. It reminded me of the words of the great pioneer missionary to Africa, Robert Moffat. *"I have seen, at different times, the smoke of a thousand villages—villages whose people are without Christ, without God, and without hope in the world ... The smoke of a thousand villages ... The smoke of a thousand villages."* Those words now became images burned into my heart.

I heard the landing gear come down and knew we were just about to land. But where? All I could see were trees. Then about sixty seconds before we touched down I saw the airport. Then I felt the bump and heard the screech of the tires as they touched the runway. *Praise God! We are really here!*

Chapter
Nine

As soon as the doors opened on the plane the heat and humidity of the jungle met us like a slap in the face. Once again we were accosted by men who wanted to handle our luggage for us for a fee.

We headed out the door to a throng of people waiting to meet us. Smiling brown faces and big, bright dark brown eyes greeted us. A Peruvian man by the name of Carlos greeted us in perfect English.

"Welcome to Iquitos. My name is Carlos. I am with Clark Barnard and YWAM. This is Osmar. He works with us as a translator also," he said as he shook our hands.

We were led to a big bus. All of the luggage was placed on top. There was a lot! Eight people going into the jungle for ten days with all of our clothes, camping gear and snacks! I stood amazed watching the men handing and sometimes throwing the luggage up to the man on top as he loaded our supplies. Then it was all strapped down.

In the parking lot of the airport there was a huge billboard that read, "Iquitos, The Gateway to the Amazon." Several of us took pictures of it before we were hurried onto the bus.

It was a fifteen minute drive through the streets of Iquitos to the YWAM base. As I sat on the bus watching out the window, I had the strange feeling I had been here before. Although I had not been there before, it seemed so familiar. I had seen similar roadside tiendas, ragged old buses overfilled with people, and colorful, shanty houses side by side in Guatemala and El Salvador.

We arrived at the base. A three-story yellow stucco building. We were met at the gate by a man named Julio and his wife, Yolanda, whom everyone called Yola. Neither of them spoke a word of English. There was an American living on the base named Rob. We were also blessed to have a young Mexican lady named Carmen who spoke quite a bit of English.

After we were taken to our dorms we were gathered together for a meeting. Julio addressed the team and introduced the YWAM staff and volunteers. He introduced Yola, as his wife and cook, but we would soon learn she did so much more than that. He gave us an agenda for the ten days. Then he said he wanted to share from his heart. Carlos translated as Julio talked.

Julio knew this was our first time to the jungle. As a matter of fact, there had not been many teams before us. So, he told us some things we could expect out of the trip. He also said that if we would listen to what he told us he promised to bring us safely out of the jungle. We had the opportunity to ask some questions and then the meeting was over.

During the meeting it was explained that due to the number of people on the team and only one boat to transport us all that most of the YWAM staff would have to leave a day early and travel 22 hours up the river on a river boat. The four of us ladies wanted to go with them. After some debate, it was decided that we could go. We were so excited. It was going to give us the chance to see things along the way and sleep in a hammock on the deck of the boat. We would leave that night for the docks and board the Eduardo V.

Carlos and Osmar had gone early and saved our places together on the third deck of the Eduardo. They set up many of our hammocks for us to save our places. The boat would fill up fast. The deck was covered with the sides open for breeze. They had flaps they would lower in case of rain.

Around eight o'clock the lancha, as it is called in the jungle, pulled away from the docks. The guys had come down to see us off. Bro. Butch was not in agreement with Charlene being separated from him and riding on the slow boat without him. He said he was instructed by their pastor to watch over her and bring her back safe. Charlene informed him she would be fine and rode with us despite his objections. All the guys wanted to ride the speed boat the next day and make the trip in just over four hours.

We waved goodbye to the guys and stood along the railing watching Iquitos get smaller and smaller. It was already dark as we left so we could not see anything along the way. All we could see was the silhouette of the trees moving along the distance. We would have to wait until daybreak to see the jungle.

So the four of us ladies moved back to the rear of the boat and sat along the railing in plastic chairs from the kitchen. We sat with our feet up on the rails and sang. We were all so blessed to be in the jungle. To be on that boat floating down the Amazon River. It was a dream come true for most of us.

Charlene and Carmen ended up in the kitchen sharing the call of God on their lives and the vision He had given to them for missions. Lottie, Diane and I stayed up most of the night talking and singing praises along the railing. It was loud back there due to engine so we knew we would not be disturbing anyone. Finally, at about 2:00 in the morning Lottie and Diane said they were going to their hammocks to get some rest. I decided to stay up a while longer.

When I found myself alone the realization hit me. *I am really here. I am floating down the Amazon River.* I began to cry. I was shaking from the inside out. I was so overcome by emotions. The dream that Dad and I had was coming true. I cried out to God because I knew no one could hear me over the roar of the engines.

"Thank you. Thank you. Thank you, Father!" I cried. "Thank you for giving me this privilege to be here in the Amazon. Thank you for allowing me to bring your love and Word to these people."

Once again, I thought of the words Robert Moffat said to David Livingston. *"I have seen, at different times, the smoke of a thousand villages—villages whose people are without Christ, without God, and without hope in the world."*

As I sat there and cried, thanking God for being there, I reached inside my blouse over my heart and pulled out the picture of Dad that I had been carrying with me. *We made it, Dad. We're finally here.* I knew he was with me. I could feel him with me. He was looking down from heaven with his blue eyes smiling. I feel certain he knew I was there.

We stopped at different villages along the way. Even in the middle of the night. We docked, cargo was unloaded and passengers got off. Then we pulled away and continued our travel up river.

About 4:00 in the morning I went to my hammock. I laid there swinging in my hammock watching the jungle silhouette go by. It was so relaxing. I wanted to rest but not go to sleep. I wanted to make sure I was awake to watch the sun rise on the Amazon River. I wanted to see all I could see as we traveled up the river.

I dozed off and on a little for about an hour. Then I could see that the horizon was getting brighter. Daybreak would soon be upon us. I jumped up and got out my camera. I returned to the chairs sitting along the railing. I knew the others wanted to witness sunrise, too. So, I watched and waited. I began to see the trees as we floated past them. I began to see small canoes with fishermen in them along the banks. It was time to get the others up.

I went to the hammocks where my teammates were sleeping. I softly told them it was almost sunrise. They hopped up and got their cameras too. We went to the back of the boat again. Just about the time we got there we saw a dolphin jumping right behind the boat. Wow! We had been told about the Amazon River dolphin, but now we were seeing it with our own eyes. There were two of them. We tried, but we just couldn't get a picture of them. They were too fast.

Just then the sun rose and everyone started snapping pictures. We all wanted to record our first Amazon Sunrise. It was beautiful. The sparkle of the sunlight on the water. The beam of sunlight through the dense trees. It was all so moving.

Breakfast was being served in the kitchen dining room. It was scrambled eggs and ham. Fresh fruit, orange juice and coffee. There was also toast and strawberry preserves. I had the scrambled eggs and fresh fruit with orange juice. I have never been a coffee drinker.

After breakfast we changed our clothes, brushed our teeth with bottled water and freshened our hair and makeup. We weren't sure exactly when the guys would be passing us in the speedboat, but we wanted to keep an eye out for them. We had walkie talkies that I had brought from home to communicate with each other.

About 11:00 we saw them. I had forgotten to turn my walkie talkie on. I saw Bro Butch hanging the walkie talkie out the window waving it around. That was his way of telling me to turn it on. I did. He wanted to talk to Charlene and make sure she was all right. We talked for a few minutes until they got out of range. It would be another three hours before we would catch up with them in the village where we were supposed to meet. San Miguel. That was to be the first village where we would hold a medical clinic and campaign.

Chapter
Ten

Carlos let us know to take down our hammocks and pack up things as we approached San Miguel. The guys were already there. We could see in the distance a crowd of men, women and children standing on the top of the bank. They began to wave as we approached. They were the villagers of San Miguel welcoming us to their community.

The captain slowly and meticulously guided the lancha to shore. We hit the bank with a gentle thud. A few other people, besides the YWAM team, disembarked as we did. The crew of the Eduardo V helped us unload our gear. In addition to the food and water for the team for the next ten days, we had sound equipment for the evangelistic campaigns, medical equipment and medicines. There was a large amount of cargo to unload. Much of it was rather heavy.

This was the dry season. It had not rained in weeks. The Marañon River, just like the Amazon, was extremely low. We had a climb of about thirty feet up the side of the riverbank, loaded down with supplies. The air was hot and humid. The Amazon sun felt like it was sitting on top of our heads.

By the time I reached the top, I was gasping for breath. Perspiration was running down my blood red face and neck. I made it, though. Then, I was informed it was about a half-mile trek down the path to the village. *Please, God, give me strength.* I prayed silently.

We were told to just follow the path and it would lead us to the village. "Stay on the path and watch out for snakes," someone warned us. *Seriously?* I was still trying to get my respirations back to normal as I set off for the village. My legs were already shaking from the climb up the hill. Extreme heat and humidity, excessive perspiration, heaving breathing, and lack of water meant instant dehydration. Dehydration meant headache, leg cramps and tingling, lightheadedness and nausea.

Each step I took I prayed for strength to take another one. I wanted to sit down and cry, but I couldn't. I had to go on. *I can't quit. I prayed for years for this opportunity. Now I am here. I can't fail. Father God, please give me strength.*

Walking down that path with the aspect of snakes lying in wait to prey upon us played with our imaginations. Suddenly, Carmen stepped on a stick that instantly bounced up and wrapped around her leg. She jumped and let out a blood-curdling scream. When she did, we all did. When we realized that it was just a stick that had attacked Carmen and not a real snake, everyone laughed. The children of the village who followed us especially found it funny. We laughed the rest of the way down the path and into the village.

The next thing I knew we were at the village and taken to the hut where were would be spending the next two nights. I had received the strength to take another step. I had received the strength to make it the half-mile to the village. The strength came with the laughter. I got the revelation of Nehemiah 8:10. "… for the joy of the Lord is your strength." That laughter, that joy gave me strength. That strength carried me to the village. I am sure I was not the only one in need of strength at that moment. Not the only one who needed joy. It was not the only time during that trip that joy and strength would come.

It was decided that the four of us American ladies would put up our hammocks in the same hut and stay together. This hut belonged to a family of four. It was about eight feet off the ground. The main hut was made up of three rooms. One room was the mom and dad's bedroom. One room was the two daughters' bedroom. The bedrooms were separated by a larger room that was opened in the front. The front had railing around it.

Lottie took the front because it was open and she figured it would be cooler. So she hung her hammock there next to the railing. Diane hung hers next to Lottie. Charlene's was next, and finally I hung my hammock next to the door. I was the furthest away from the open air.

We wondered, as we hung all four of our hammocks on the same supporting beam, if that was a good idea. We were all pretty hefty American ladies. Was this little flimsy beam going to hold all of our weight? That night the answer came.

After we all got our hammocks hung it was time for dinner. Yola had prepared the evening meal in the kitchen of the hut next door. The village had a pastor that Julio and the YWAM team had ministered to and helped establish him as pastor. They did not have a church building yet, though. So, after dinner we were going to hold services outside. We would just string the lights we brought and hook the lights, sound system and electrical instruments up to the generator. Bro. Butch was going to give the message that night and a couple of the team members were going to share their testimonies.

Before the service, however, a few of us ladies were in desperate need of a toilet. We were told that this village had bathrooms at the school, but the school was quite a distance away at the far end of the village. However, we were told that the pastor had an outhouse a few yards back into the jungle. Great! We would use the outhouse. It was close.

It was almost dark so we needed to hurry. One of the pastor's daughters volunteered to show us the way. She was a cute little girl of about eight years of age. She led the way. We all stuck close together. It was a little further back that we expected. There in the middle of the jungle was a little makeshift outhouse. It was made of wood that was almost rotted away in places. The "door" was a sheet of dirty, ragged cloth. Diane was the first to venture in. She moved away the cloth and said, "Uh, I think someone stole the toilet."

"What?" We all asked. We looked in. There was no toilet. Just a hole dug in the dirt floor with two small pieces of wood across either side of the hole.

"That IS the toilet!" I said laughing.

"What?" Diane asked. "How do I use that?"

"Put one foot on one side and the other on the other side, drop your pants and assume the position." I said giggling. I had been in outhouses like this in Guatemala before.

"Oooh, Girl! Huh uh. I don't think I can do that."

"What choice do you have?"

"Come on. You can do it!" the others encouraged.

Well, she did it. It was a little awkward, but she prevailed. Next, it was Charlene's turn. She went in and drew closed the cloth door. Within about thirty seconds we heard a crack and Charlene holler, "Oh, no. I just broke their toilet!"

She barely got her pants up when she came out the door. We looked in. One of the pieces of boards was broken and had fallen into the hole. Charlene shared how her foot fell into the hole but she pulled it out quickly before she stepped in all of the …well, you know. We all started laughing. Just then the pastor's daughter started running back to her hut.

"Oh, no! She's running to tell on us."

Lottie and I hurried and used it and we all headed back to the pastor's hut to see what was said. Expecting to be in trouble for breaking the toilet, we were greeted with inquiries as to our well being. Yes, yes, we were all right. With Carmen translating, Charlene apologized for causing damage to the toilet. The pastor said it was no problem. The boards were old and rotted and needed to be replaced anyhow.

It was now dark and the music team began praise and worship. The sound of the music drew a crowd of people from the village. As we sat under the lights strung above us we had to fight off all the bugs. It was hard to praise the Lord and clap while swatting away the bugs. It wasn't just a zillion mosquitoes. There were many other unidentified insects buzzing around our heads and diving at us. We were wearing 100% DEET and covered as much exposed skin as possible, but the heat and humidity made wearing extra clothes unbearable. Some of us stood in the back away from the lights so the bugs would leave us alone.

Brother Butch delivered an awesome message that included his testimony. It was a very powerful message of God's delivering power. A couple of other team members greeted the people and gave brief testimonies. Carlos did an awesome job of translating for us. Several responded to prayer and received Jesus that night.

It was now time to head to the hut and get into our hammocks. We ladies decided it would be a good idea to go to the outhouse one last time before bed. The trek through the jungle to the outhouse was now completely dark. The idea of snakes at our feet or hanging in the trees above us made us little bit nervous. We had a plan. We walked back to back down the path. We were all armed with flashlights. The one in front aimed the light on the path in front to make sure it was clear of snakes. The one on either side watched the sidelines for snakes. The one in back was in charge of monitoring the branches above us.

It was slow going and we all had the nervous giggles. Success! We all made it. With bladders emptied and no fatalities from snakebites we made it back to our hut. Our task was completed. Now for a peaceful night's rest. Lottie stopped to visit with the family whose hut we were staying in. She was fluent in Spanish. Up the steps of the hut the rest of us went. I was first. I came to my hammock first since it was by the door.

As soon as I shined my flashlight on my hammock I froze in my tracks. I gasped. "Oh, my Gosh!"

"What? What is it?" The others asked.

"Look!"

The other ladies followed the beam of my flashlight to see what I was looking at. "Oh, no!" There, hanging on the side of my hammock by the zipper where I get in was the ugliest frog I had ever seen. It was translucent. You could almost see its insides. "Is it poisonous?" one of them asked.

"I have no idea, but I am not about to touch it and find out."

Just then we heard a familiar voice outside talking to Carmen who was hanging in her hammock underneath us. It was Dr. Bob. "Dr. Bob!" we all screamed. "Help!" He came running up the steps with his newly purchased machete in hand.

"What's wrong?" he asked with genuine concern in his voice.

"Look!" we all said in unison.

He turned his head in the direction of the light and saw the frog. He raised his machete high.

"Wait!" I hollered.

"What? Why?"

"I need a picture!"

"Oh, my gosh, JoJo. Really?" Charlene asked.

"Yes. I need to show everyone back home what was hanging on my hammock."

I got my picture and then said, "Ok, Dr. Bob, kill it!"

Once again he raised his machete high. "Wait!" I hollered again.

"Now what?" they all asked.

"Dr. Bob, don't cut up my hammock. It is all I brought to sleep in." I just imagined him hacking my hammock to pieces during his frog slaying endeavor.

"I won't. I promise to be careful."

He poked it with the tip of his machete. It didn't budge. He did it again. No move. Then he tried to gently slide it off with the edge of the machete. Still nothing. That was one stubborn frog. Then, suddenly, it jumped. So did we. We screamed. The frog hit the floor and we went scurrying away bumping into each other and screaming.

"What is going on up there?" Carmen asked from below.

"A big ugly frog!" someone shouted. Carmen broke out it a roar of laughter. "It's not funny." I said. "It could be poisonous!"

Finally, Dr. Bob shoved it out the door with his machete and the impending or at least the perceived danger was over. I thanked him for his help and he left. Charlene, Diane and I began to get ready for bed and settle in to our hammocks for the night.

I unzipped my hammock and gently slid in. This was the first time any of us had to sleep in our hammocks with the mosquito nets zipped. I got situated in and zipped up the net. As I laid there I could feel my temperature rising. I was already hot and wet from perspiration. With the mosquito net zipped there was absolutely no airflow. I was tucked back in the corner away from the open air. Suddenly, I felt like my insides were on fire.

I had a little six-inch battery operated fan with me. I turned it on and blew it right in my face. I felt as though I was going to pass out from the heat. As a nurse, I knew I was nearing heat exhaustion. I began to pray. I knew that if not dealt with it could turn to heat stroke. I shut my eyes and took long deep breaths with the fan sitting on my chest blowing directly in my face. *Oh, Jesus, please help me. I do not want to die here. Please send a cooling breeze. Help me cool down.* I prayed to myself.

Mom was struggling with idea of me in the jungle. This was difficult for her. As my pastor she knew it was God that I go to the Amazon, but it was difficult for her as a mother. After all, she lost her husband ten years earlier to malaria in the jungles of Africa. Now I prayed that she would not lose her daughter too.

Soon, Lottie came up and asked what all the commotion was about earlier. We began to tell her about the incident with the frog as she got ready for bed and climbed into her hammock. Diane had gotten out of her hammock when Lottie came in, and starting fidgeting with it. We could feel our hammocks shake.

"Diane, what are you doing?" Lottie asked.

"Something just didn't feel right with my hammock, so I am adjusting it."

"What was wrong with it?"

"Well, I think it was uneven and it was sagging too much," she said as she tightened the straps that connected to the beam on the wall. Soon she was done messing with it and headed back to bed.

We heard the zipper unzip. Suddenly we heard a swoosh just as Diane hollered, "Aahhhhh!" Then we heard a thud.

"Diane, are you all right?" we all said through uncontrollable laughter. Even Carmen was laughing below us. "Diane?" No answer. Just laughing. Finally, we stopped laughing. Maybe Diane was really hurt. Maybe she knocked herself out. We hadn't heard from her since the thud.

Charlene grabbed her flashlight and shined it in the direction of Diane's hammock. She had to lower the beam of light. Finally, she saw the hammock turned upside down. There, sitting on the roof of her hammock, on the floor of the hut was Diane. She was conscious. She was laughing, but not a sound came out. Her body was shaking from laughing, but no sound was coming out.

Charlene and Lottie got out of their hammocks and helped Diane put her hammock back up and get safely back in it. I was still struggling with the heat. Everyone was hot, but for some reason I really thought I was going to pass out from heat exhaustion. I had really gotten overheated. I felt bad that I didn't get out to help, but the ladies assured me it was well under control and there was nothing really I could do.

When all was quiet again and everyone safe in their hammocks, we asked Lottie to share a devotion with us. She did and then we all closed in prayer. Afterwards, Lottie said something that opened our eyes. "You know, ladies, that frog didn't get up here on JoJo's hammock by itself."

"What do you mean, Lottie?" we asked.

"Someone purposely put it there while we were in service."

"But why would they do that?" I asked.

"Not everyone is happy that we are here. They are especially not happy that we are sharing the Gospel with them. You have to remember there is a lot of witchcraft here in the jungle. I believe someone was trying to put a spell on us and drive us out of here."

"Whoa. I never thought of that," I said soberly.

"Neither did I," Diane whispered.

Sometime in the middle of the night the temperature dropped enough to allow my core temperature to cool. I drifted off to sleep and woke up with the sound of crowing roosters. It is "early to bed and early to rise" in the jungle. We were to have breakfast and devotions next door, and then carry the supplies down to the other end of the village to the schoolhouse. That is where we would hold the clinic.

During breakfast we found out that I was not the only one who struggled with the extreme heat that night. The guys, Jimmy, Randy, Jim Tomlinson and Dr. Bob were staying in a building a few huts down that had a metal roof. It got so hot in there that all of the guys were drenched with sweat and beginning to dehydrate. They got little to no sleep that night. They thought they would die, too. They were making plans to sleep somewhere else tonight. Even if it meant sleeping outside!

We set up four stations with a nurse at three of them and Jim Tomlinson (J. T.) at the fourth one. He was a physician's assistant. Each station was assigned a translator. Carmen translated for Charlene. Carlos translated for Diane. Osmar translated for J.T. and Lottie translated for me. Lottie had been a missionary to El Salvador for twelve years at that time and was fluent in Spanish.

We saw about 110 people in the village that day. There were a wide variety of illnesses, but nearly everyone had parasites. We soon learned that parasites were the number one problem and the biggest killer of children in the Amazon. Upper respiratory problems were second. Most of us had worked together before with Mercy Mission Teams in other countries so we flowed together well. The clinic lasted several hours.

We ended up staying another night in San Miguel. That afternoon a small team would travel to the next village and hold a brief clinic. The village was extremely small but they were sick and needed attention too. Charlene was on that team. When they returned she shared how they had to get out of the speedboat and carry the supplies across the sandy beach. It was quite a distant across the beach to the village. She shared the details of some of the people they saw and the illnesses they treated.

That night we held another service outdoors. Same setup. Music. Testimonies. Sharing the Word of God. Lights. Bugs! Oh, well, it was the jungle, after all. Dr. Bob shared the Word that second night. Once again, several responded to prayer and accepted Jesus. It was a great time of fellowship with our new brothers and sisters in the Lord.

We went back to our hut, stopping off at the jungle outhouse along the way. When we got to the hut we found the guys setting up their hammocks. They were joining Carmen underneath the hut. We warned a couple of them that they might want to move to another location under the hut. When we were asked why they should move we told them. The lady of the house sleeps directly above here and gets up in the middle of the night, squats over that hole in the floor and urinates. We found evidence of it that morning we when got up. Needless to say, they heeded our advice and moved!

After saying good night we headed up the steps to our hammocks. It was a bit slight cooler tonight. Still hot and humid, but not as bad as the night before. One by one we got into our hammocks. Once again, Diane was the last one in after making a few adjustments to her hammock.

Suddenly, there was a crash. It was not Diane's hammock this time. We all jumped up. It was the wall that the beam we attached our hammocks to held up. It gave way under our weight and the wall came crashing down. Thank God it was not a main supporting beam to the hut. We could have brought the entire hut down.

Working together, we were able to get the wall back up and anchored with some rope I happened to bring with me. After a few minutes, the wall was back up and we were back in our hammocks. No real damage done. We endured some teasing and a few jokes the next morning at breakfast when we explained what the noise was the guys heard in the middle of the night. Yes, we ladies really knew how to bring the house down!

Chapter
Eleven

I mmediately following breakfast and devotions, we loaded into a dugout canoe with a small engine that looked like it belonged on a lawn mower. The engine was on one end of a long metal pole and on the other end was a small propeller. Dugout canoes with these special engines were called "peque peques." They were called this because everyone said that was the sound they made as they traveled along the river.

The luggage, camping gear and medical supplies were loaded into the peque peque. The YWAM team rode in it, too. Yola, Carlos and the Mercy Mission Team rode in the speedboat driven by Julio. Our captain. The peque peque was much slower than the speedboat, which had a 60 horse power engine. It was made of lightweight aluminum. The peque peque was sent on ahead to the next village while we said goodbye to the people of San Miguel.

Within a short period of time we were loaded in the boat and on our way to the village of San Martin. This was quite a contrast to the boat ride we ladies had on the way to San Miguel.

We took the twenty-two hour lancha ride there. Now we were blasting our way through the waters in a speedboat. It was definitely much cooler with the wind whipping through our hair.

Within thirty minutes we were overtaking the peque peque with our YWAM team members and all of our gear. We waved and hollered at the team as we buzzed by them. However, just another thirty minutes up river they would catch up to us. Due to the low level of the river we suddenly got stuck on a sand bar. Julio had to shut off the engine. Julio and Carlos then grabbed paddles from under the front row of seats and began to paddle us off the sand bar and into deeper waters.

Strangely enough the deeper waters were close to shore while the sand bar was in the middle of the river. This was a very slow and tedious process. We had now been out on the river for over an hour and stuck for the last thirty minutes. It began to get hotter and hotter. We were no longer being kept cool by the wind from traveling at 40 miles an hour. The Amazon sun was beating down. The metal roof of that metal boat acted as an oven, reflecting heat upon those of us inside.

We were now fairly close to shore but in the midst of a bunch of reeds. The reeds were very dense. We were in deeper water now but because of the reeds Julio could not use the motor. The reeds would wrap around the propeller and burn up the engine. He and Carlos would have to continue to paddle until we got past these reeds.

Lottie had brought old-fashioned baby diapers from El Salvador. She gave each of us ladies one to tie around our necks or use as "sweat rags." I untied mine from around my neck and dipped it down in the water. As I was dipping it up and down in the water, Julio suddenly turned around and yelled something back at me. Carlos quickly translated.

"JoJo, no! Don't put your hands in the water!"

"Ok. I'm sorry," I said as I jerked my hand and the diaper out of the water.

"Julio apologized for yelling at you, but he said to tell everyone to keep their hands inside the boat while we are here in these reeds. This is feeding grounds for Caiman alligators and anacondas," he kindly explained.

As he spoke those words I quickly slid myself in closer to the center of the boat. I noticed all of us ladies did. Some of the men did too. I asked Carlos to thank Julio for me. He did and Julio turned around and flashed me a smile. I wasn't upset because he yelled at me. I understood why he did. I was thankful that he did.

Sitting directly behind me was Randy Miller. Good ol' fun-loving Randy! Randy had reached over and snapped a piece of one of the reeds off when no one was looking. He then decided to slowly run it along the back of my neck. Thinking an anaconda was wrapping itself around my neck, I jumped up screaming and almost capsized the boat. Once again, Julio turned around yelling. Once again, it was me that was causing the problem.

"Sit down, JoJo! You're going to tip us over," Carlos said, translating Julio's warning.

"I'm sorry. I thought an anaconda was wrapping around my neck," I said apologetically as I slunk down in my seat wanting to suddenly disappear.

"Sorry, JoJo," Randy whispered, feeling badly for what he had done.

Needless to say the rest of the trip to San Martin was rather quiet and uneventful. No one said hardly a word.

After unloading our gear, we were escorted by the village leader to a "lodge" where we would be staying for a couple of nights. The lodge was rather humble. It was screened in, but there were many holes and openings where mosquitoes could get in. There was a dining room area that had a couple of picnic tables pushed together. We ladies were going to hang our hammocks in the dining room and sleep there.

There were four bedrooms in the lodge too. Two of the rooms had twin beds on either side of the room. One room had bunk beds on either side of the room. The fourth room had a double bed. Julio and Yola slept in the double bed. The other beds were filled up with the rest of the male members of Mercy Mission Team and Carlos. The YWAM staff, except for Carmen, slept in pup tents in the foyer. Carmen was in the dining room with us ladies.

There was still a little daylight left after we got settled into the lodge so we all took a walk around the village to meet the people and enjoy the beautiful evening. San Martin was a tourist village setup to attract tourists on riverboat tours. Across the river was a place set up for jungle tours. Given the fact this was a tourist village, it had a couple of tiendas that sold cold bottled water, soda pop and snacks. The tiendas also carried a few needed items like toothbrushes and batteries.

There was a sidewalk around the entire village, which was about two and a half times the size of the first village where we stayed. There was also electricity in this village. Now, they only had electricity from about 6:00 in the evening until 9:00. Then the entire village went to bed. Bright and early, before daybreak, the entire village was up and working.

It was an absolutely beautiful evening. Parrots were chirping loudly. Children were running and playing. Many of the children were splashing in the water as we walked along the river. When we got up to the center of the village a woman who said she was the pastor of a large church there in San Martin met us. She shook hands with Dr. Bob and invited us to stay with her in her church. She began to follow us around.

I really did not know why, but this woman gave me the creeps. I stayed away from her as much as I could. She just made me very uncomfortable. A few of us ladies sat down on the top of a wooden fishing boat that was turned upside down. The woman pastor joined us. She sat right next to Charlene.

Later, Charlene shared with me that once when she turned to smile at the pastor, she growled at her. Charlene said she knew immediately that the so-called lady "pastor" was possessed.

We noticed that the pastora, which is what women pastors are called in latin countries, never prayed for any of her church members.

She never prayed for anyone for that matter. We soon learned that she preyed upon them instead.

The sun was now setting over the Marañon. It was the most beautiful sunset I had ever seen. Most of us were taking pictures of it. It was absolutely breathtaking. I stood in awe of God's handiwork for several minutes. No one could ever have painted such a magnificent work of art more beautiful than that sunset. Once again I was overcome with emotions at the realization that I was living a dream. I was standing on the banks of the Marañon in the midst of the Amazon Jungle. I was instantly aware of my father's presence again as I stood there giving thanks to God for allowing me the privilege of being there. I praised Him for the fulfillment of a lifelong dream that originated from Him in the first place.

It was now time for dinner. Yola would be serving it in the dining room of the lodge. We just raised our hammocks up out of the way and sat around the table together. The dinner was served. Fish. Everyone was thrilled. Everyone except Randy and I that is. Randy or I neither one eat fish. As a matter of fact, I don't eat seafood of any kind. I don't believe there is much of it that Randy eats either. I ate a few cucumber slices. I excused myself from the table. Randy wasn't at the table. He went to his room to fix himself some dinner. He brought instant meals. He was heating up some basil chicken on his mini propane stove. Now that was planning ahead!

I had some snacks in my bag. I had brought some crackers and beef jerky. Charlene introduced me to Pistachios. Diane pulled out individual packets of Spam amongst a myriad of other goodies, including peanut butter. Several of us had brought water flavor packets like Crystal light. After the evening meal we all pulled our goodies out and combined them. We had a bounty of goods.

We also pooled things like batteries, toilet paper, soap and shampoo, bug spray, flashlights and rain gear. You name it. We had it. We realized that at any given time on the trip, if somebody needed something, somebody had it to give. We had all things in common and every need was met. Just like in the Bible!

Outside, behind the dining room, were two bathrooms. That meant there were two stalls. Each had a commode. No toilet seat, just the toilet. There was no running water; so in order to flush you filled up a bucket with water from the barrel beside the toilet. A drainpipe, which caught rainwater from the roof and dumped it into the barrel, kept the barrel full. Again, the door was a sheet of plastic nailed up to the frame of the doorway.

We had service that night at a small church that was recently established. The pastora insisted that we hold service at her church. Julio, graciously declined. He had given his word to the other pastor. None of us had a good feeling about the pastora. Although we actually had a building to hold service in that night, the order of the service was the same. There was praise and worship, announcements and offering, team introduction, testimonies and presentation of the Word. Lottie brought forth a powerful message that night.

After we got back to the lodge and were laying in our hammocks, Lottie shared with us that delivering the message was like "plowing ground." She said she could sense a real heavy oppression. There was a demonic stronghold somewhere. She said we needed to agree together in prayer that the clinic in the morning would be different. That the stronghold would be broken and that lives would be set free by the power of God. "Amen!" we all agreed and began to intercede for the next day's clinic.

The clinic was held in a structure that was just a wooden floor with a thatched roof over it held up by six wooden poles. It was about four feet off the ground. It was nice because it was open all around and therefore allowed for a breeze. It was much cooler than the closed in school building the day before with the metal roof.

The clinic went pretty well. There were a lot of sick people but nothing really major. Many of the same illnesses as the village before. Cough and colds. Upper respiratory infections. Body aches and pains. Of course, the number one problem was parasites. There was a minor injury here and there also.

Then Dr. Bob said, "Mercy Team, gather around. We have a real sick little girl here." At his feet was a little girl wrapped in towels. She was brought to the clinic by her grandparents. The grandfather laid her on the floor and walked away. The grandmother sat on the floor next to her. Lottie began asking the grandmother questions for us to try and figure out what was wrong with her.

As Lottie talked, Charlene and I began to unwrap the little girl. What we saw broke our hearts. This little girl was all shriveled up. Muscle atrophy had begun. She was all drawn up. It was as though the little girl had cerebral palsy. She could not move. Her eyes were matted together and flies and gnats were eating at the exudate that ran from them. Her little body was covered all over with scabies.

Charlene and I began to work together to cleanse her eyes and wash her little dirty body. We prayed as we touched her and cleaned her up. I could tell the rest of the team was standing around us praying for this little girl. We kept working on getting her eyes opened and cleaning her up as Lottie began to relay the story that her grandmother told.

Just six weeks earlier she was a healthy little girl. She would run and play with the rest of the children. Then suddenly she began to grow weak and fall down. Within just a few days she was totally paralyzed. The grandmother said that her daughter, the little girl's mother, had been involved with a very evil man. His family had put a curse on the little girl. She shared that when her daughter saw what was happening to her little girl she just ran away. No one had seen her since. Now the grandparents were left to care for this little girl.

Lottie laid her hand on the little girl and started patting her as she prayed. Then she looked up at us and said, "I really believe this is demonic. I believe the evil the man was involved in and the curse he put upon her has taken a toll on this little one. I believe this is more demonic than disease." So we all prayed for deliverance for the little girl as well as healing. Charlene had a bottle of anointing oil she had brought. She felt impressed to pour it all over the little girl and pray the curse would be broken, that she would be set free.

We got her eyes open after we cleaned all of the infection away. I rinsed her eyes with a saline solution after they were cleaned. We didn't have any antibiotic drops to put in them. She had such beautiful big dark brown eyes. She was searching our eyes with hers. I am sure she was searching for some answers. She was trying to communicate with us with her eyes. As we prayed she began to wiggle a finger. Then she moved a hand and a foot a little bit. It was as if she was trying to move. To get her little body to do what it couldn't do before. She began to make some noises with her mouth as if she was trying to tell us something.

We prayed and worked on the little girl for about an hour. She seemed better when her grandfather carried her away. She was clean. Her eyes were open and they were clean. She was moving things she couldn't before. All we could do was believe for a miracle. We had to leave her in God's Hands. We asked Him for a healing, restorative miracle. As we left that village the next day, we thanked God that He was healing her. We wanted so badly to be able to go back to that village the next year and see her running around and playing again with the other children.

We held clinics in a couple more villages and spent the night in them. Now it was time to head to a larger village called Santa Rita de Castilla. The villages we had been in on this trip were in a region of the Amazon called the Pacaya Samiria National Reserve. It was a wildlife reserve area. It was absolutely beautiful, but the people were very sick. Santa Rita de Castilla was going to be our last village before heading back to Iquitos. Our first trip to the Amazon was almost over.

Chapter
Twelve

Santa Rita de Castilla was a very big village. It had a clinic, but it was empty. There was no one there to run it. The village had sidewalks all around it. It had several large tiendas with cold pop and bottled water. Instead of staying in huts, and hanging in our hammocks, we would be staying in a hospedaje. Those were small motels, but with no bathrooms or lobby. Just rooms with beds. Nothing more.

Some of us got our own rooms, while others had two twin beds in their room. The rooms were very small. There was just enough room for a twin bed, or two, with a mosquito net over each bed and a nightstand next to the beds.

The clinic would be held the next morning in a big concrete building used for village meetings or gatherings. They had just put kerosene on the floors. They did that to keep the mosquitoes down. The only thing it really did was make it stink and very slippery. It was like a skating rink in there. It also made it extremely flammable!

The clinic was soon underway and things were progressing well. Once again we treated everyone in the village over a year old with parasite medicine, except for pregnant women. We also had the typical cough and colds, upper respiratory infections, aches and pains and symptoms of dehydration. The dehydration was usually a result of diarrhea from the parasites, lack of drinking enough water and being in the sun all day working in the fields.

Close to the end of the clinic, a young mother came in with an infant in her arms and two other children. The oldest was an eight-year-old girl who looked like she was nine months pregnant. The whites of her eyes were completely yellow. This little girl was in liver failure. But why? What caused one so young to be in complete liver failure?

The little girl's mom began to tell us that a doctor who occasionally went from village to village saw the little girl and told her it was parasites. He gave her a handful of little pills and said she would be fine. It seemed either the doctor had no idea what it was or that he just didn't care and was telling the mother what she wanted to hear. He gave her false hope. We felt compelled to tell the mother the truth.

The truth was without a miracle from God this little girl was going to die. It broke the mother's heart. It did ours too. We all gathered around and just as we did for the little girl in San Martin, we prayed for a miracle. We asked God to heal her and restore her health. There was nothing that man could for this little one. It was too late. Only God could help her. Once again we wished we could return there and see what God had done for this little girl too.

The clinic was over. It was time to head back to Iquitos. Again, we would have to send the gear, luggage and YWAM team back on the Eduardo. The speedboat with Mercy Team would leave in the morning. We ladies were definitely going with them. This time because of the stories we told the guys, some the guys wanted to go with us on the lancha. We packed up all of our belongings and headed down to the river. Those that would leave tomorrow joined us at the river. We were not sure exactly what time the lancha would be by, but we needed to be ready.

It was a beautiful evening. Many of the village children hung out by the river with us and played. It was a good sixty feet down to the river from the top of the bank where we waited. The river had fallen that much during the nine days we were out in the river communities. Some of the fishermen had dug steps in the dirt to make it a little easier to get up and down. All of our gear was sitting in a pile at the top of the bank. There was nothing left for us to do, but wait for the Eduardo.

Soon the evening sky became dark. Ominous looking clouds were moving closer to us. We could see lightning in the distance as well. In the rainforest you can see rain for miles. It looked like a curtain drawn across the Marañon River. We could see it moving quickly in our direction. We grabbed our personal belongings and ran for cover under the overhang of the village clinic. The clinic was full of medical equipment and pharmaceuticals but closed up tight because there was no doctor or medical personnel to run it.

We stood under the protection of the eaves waiting for the Eduardo to come. We were hoping that the rain would stop before it came so we could load ourselves and gear without getting wet. We would soon learn that getting wet was the least of our worries.

After two hours of torrential rain, we saw the lights of the Eduardo in the distance. Still the rain came down in buckets. We waited as it approached. Finally, a man in the village came up to Julio and gave him the bad news. Julio spoke with Carlos who then translated the bad news to us. The Eduardo was not stopping. The rains had washed the dock away and made it difficult for them to stop there. If we wanted a ride, we would have to board it out in the middle of the Marañon.

In order to do this, it meant loading ourselves and our gear in a peque peque and heading out to meet it. We didn't have a choice. So we grabbed our belongings and headed to the top of the bank to walk down the makeshift steps to the peque peque below us. The Eduardo would cut off her engine and ride the current until we boarded.

As we reached the top of the bank the guys said, "Go ahead, JoJo, you go first." I did. I took one step and my feet went out from under me. The steps were gone. Washed out by the torrential rain. I began to roll down the hill toward the river. I picked up speed as I went. The thought went through my head: *if I hit the river I am gone! I will be washed out into the river and never seen again.* The current of the Amazon and Marañon Rivers was very strong.

"Jesus! Save me!" I cried out as I rolled down the hill ever closer to the river.

Suddenly, I rolled into the legs of a man standing on the side of the bank. I had rolled about two thirds of the way down. When I hit his legs it stopped me. He reached down and with one hand and one quick swoop picked me up and stood me on my feet. I no sooner stood upright on my feet than Dr. Bob, Jimmy and Randy reached me.

"JoJo, are you all right?"

"Yes, thank you. If it hadn't been for this man standing here though, I would not be."

"What man?" they asked.

"This ma-a," I stopped. There was no one there. "Well, the man that was standing here. I rolled into his legs and it stopped me from going on down. He reached down and picked me up."

"JoJo, there was no man standing here. We had our flashlights on you the whole way. You just suddenly stopped and jumped up on your feet."

No, that is not what happened, but there was no time to discuss it. We had to go and go quickly. We threw our stuff in the canoe and away we went. It took two peque peques. Out into the darkness we went. In loaded down canoes. In an Amazon rainstorm. On raging waters. At the time we never thought about it. We just did what we had to do.

Finally, we caught up to the Eduardo and held on to the side of the lancha while we threw our belongings up. Then we grabbed onto hands as we climbed up the side of the lancha to the deck. Our peque peque driver steadied the canoe as we did. One by one we made it aboard. We stopped, counted to see if everyone had made it, prayed we got all of our luggage and gear and headed up to the third deck. I was covered from head to feet in mud. We were all soaked to the bone.

When we reached the third deck we all stopped and looked at each other. It suddenly hit us what just happened. We recalled the events of the past thirty minutes. Suddenly, I exclaimed, as the realization hit me, "That was so Indiana Jones!" Everyone laughed. "Yes, I suppose it was," Randy said laughing. "Only YOU, JoJo!"

I was muddy, soaked and now shivering. The only things clean or dry I had was my pajamas. As I went back in the dark to the showers to get cleaned up, the guys set my hammock up for me. When I came out my team, my new close-knit family was sitting along the railing talking. The rain had finally stopped. "Are you sure you are all right, JoJo?" Charlene asked. "Yes, I am fine. Thank God, I am fine! Now, everybody we need to talk."

We discussed for a few minutes what really happened on that hill. Everyone laughed as they said that Diane hollered, "Slow your roll, JoJo!" I never heard that because of the sound of the rain and praying out loud for Jesus to save me. But now it was funny. Everyone agreed though that there was no man standing there. They all saw in the beam of their flashlights that I was alone.

"No, I was not alone," I said reflectively. "I had my angel with me!" That was the only explanation. We all agreed God had sent an angel to my rescue. So, instead of an Indiana Jones experience, I had another close encounter of the God Kind!

Laying in my hammock that night, I thanked God for all He had done on that trip. I thanked Him first for the honor of being there.

Then thanked Him for all of the miracles He had performed for the villagers and for us. I thanked Him for divine protection that was now taking us safely back.

Back in Iquitos, on our last night there, we had a meeting and dinner. We called it the Last Supper. It was a dinner meeting that Dr. Bob had for not only all of us on the Mercy Team, but for everyone on the YWAM team that joined us on the river. This is our last dinner together before we left for the States. We got the opportunity to share together what we learned and experienced on that trip.

Remembering the words of Julio at the beginning of the trip when it was my turn to share I said, "Julio, you told us that if we would listen to you and do what you said that you would bring us back safely." He nodded his head and smiled. "Well, I want you to know that I would follow you to the ends of the earth. I trust you and God with my life."

I had no idea, in September of 2007, what would come of those words I spoke. However, soon I would find myself following Julio to what seemed to be the ends of the earth. I continue to trust Julio and God with my life.

Floating down that river, I said I would never be on, going to countries I said I would never visit, and doing things I said I would never do, I realize that it is all I desire to do. This is the reason I was born. I left a piece of my heart in the Amazon and I would find it there again the very next year.

Not the End. It's only the Beginning!

Sources

http://www.ncdc.noaa.gov/oa/reports/mitch/mitch.html

http://www.charismanow.com/index.php/component/content/article/248-people-events/663-living-water-teaching-mission-carries-on-after-plane-tragedy

About the
Author

JoeLynn Daugherty is the founder of Living Waters Medical Missions, Int'l (LWMM) and has over twenty-four years of medical missions experience. She has both led and joined medical teams to such places as Russia, Mexico, Guatemala, San Salvador, Haiti, Dominican Republic and now the Amazon Jungle of Peru. She now lives in the Amazon Jungle where she has for worked for the past eight years. JoeLynn will be ministering to the mestizo villages and primitive tribes in the Amazon River Basin of northern Peru near the borders of Brazil, Colombia and Ecuador.

JoeLynn's desire is to reach the unreached tribes tucked away in the remote areas of the Amazon Jungle. Using her nursing degree as well as her diploma from Bible College and World Missions, she intends on meeting the physical, mental and spiritual needs of the Amazon people. The recent completion of the medical boat will facilitate her efforts to go village to village with medical care, digging of wells for clean water and the Gospel of Jesus Christ.

JoeLynn has authored both Christian fiction and nonfiction books with emphasis on real life situations experienced in the jungles of Central and South America. She has a burning passion for photography and photojournalism and plans to have a photography book published soon showcasing the majesty of the people, animals and beauty of the Amazon Jungle.

For more information on the vision and ministry of JoeLynn Daugherty and LWMM please contact her at:

Living Waters Medical Missions, Int'l
P.O. Box 267
Portsmouth OH 45662
740-357-0326

or email her at:
lwmm.intl@gmail.com

or visit her website at:
www.lwmm-intl.com